Professional Scala

I0010101

Combine object-oriented and functional programming to build high-performance applications

Mads Hartmann
Ruslan Shevchenko

BIRMINGHAM - MUMBAI

Professional Scala

Acquisitions Editor: Aditya Date
Development Editor: Murtaza Haamid
Production Coordinator: Vishal Pawar

First published: July 2018

Production reference: 1300718

Published by Packt Publishing Ltd.
Livery Place, 35 Livery Street
Birmingham B3 2PB, UK.

ISBN: 978-1-78953-383-5

www.packtpub.com

https://mapt.packtpub.com/

Mapt is an online digital library that gives you full access to over 5,000 books and videos, as well as industry leading tools to help you plan your personal development and advance your career. For more information, please visit https://mapt.packtpub.com/ website.

Why Subscribe?

- Spend less time reading and more time coding with practical eBooks and Videos from over 4,000 industry professionals
- Improve your learning with Skill Plans built especially for you
- Get a free eBook or video every month
- Mapt is fully searchable
- Copy and paste, print, and bookmark content

PacktPub.com

Did you know that Packt offers eBook versions of every book published, with PDF and ePub files available? You can upgrade to the eBook version at www.PacktPub.com and as a print book customer, you are entitled to a discount on the eBook copy. Get in touch with us at service@packtpub.com for more details.

At www.PacktPub.com, you can also read a collection of free technical articles, sign up for a range of free newsletters, and receive exclusive discounts and offers on Packt books and eBooks.

Contributors

About the Authors

Mads Hartmann is a software engineer with a fondness for automation and programming languages, especially statically typed functional ones. He holds a masters degree in computer science from the University of Copenhagen and he is currently working as a full-stack engineer at Family.

He is active in the Copenhagen developer scene and he has organized a meetup group for people interested in Scala and co-organized a meetup group for people generally interested in programming languages.

Ruslan Shevchenko is a system architect and a software developer who is focused on building reliable software systems. He specializes in programming languages and frameworks such as Scala, Java (J2SE, J2EE, Android), O/R Mapping, C++ , C, JavaScript, Perl, Tcl, and TermWare.

The domains he specializes in are telecommunications, OSS/billing systems, finance, code analysis, social integration, system utilities architecture domains, large-scale software systems, and distributed processing.

In terms of architecture, his specialist domains are large-scale software systems and distributed processing.

Table of Contents

Preface

Scala is a type-safe JVM language that incorporates both object-oriented and functional programming into an extremely concise, logical, and extraordinarily powerful language. Some may be surprised to know that Scala is not quite as new as they may have thought, having first been introduced in 2003. However, it is in the past few years in particular that Scala has begun to develop a significant following.

This book enables you to build and contribute to Scala programs, recognizing common patterns and techniques used with the language.

This is a practical book which provides you with a lot of hands-on experience with Scala.

Who This Book Is For

This book is for developers who are interested in learning about the advanced features of the Scala language. Basic knowledge of the Scala programming language is required to follow the instructions in this book.

What This Book Covers

Chapter 1, Setting up the Development Environment, shows you how to set up your development environment. You'll learn the basics of Scala, such as what the simple Scala program looks like and what a typical developer flow is. It'll also cover some aspects of testing your Scala program by using unit testing.

Chapter 2, Basic Language Features, covers classes and objects, traits, pattern matching, case class, and so on. You'll also implement your chatbot application by applying the object oriented concepts.

Chapter 3, Functions, covers functional programming with Scala and how object- oriented and functional approaches complete each other. You'll identify generic classes and also identify how to create user-defined pattern matching and why is it useful.

Chapter 4, Scala Collections, teaches you how to work with lists. Then, it covers some more relevant data structures. Finally, you'll look at how collections relate to monads and how you can use that knowledge to make some powerful abstractions in your code.

Chapter 5, Scala Type System, covers the type system and polymorphism. It'll also enable you to identify the different types of variance, which provides a way to constrain parameterized types. Then, you'll cover some advanced types such as abstract type members and option.

Chapter 6, Implicits, covers implicit parameters and implicit conversions. You'll be learning about how they work, how to use them, and what kind of benefits and perils they provide.

Chapter 7, Functional Idioms, covers the core concepts of functional programming like Pure functions, immutability, and higher-order functions. It'll also cover two popular functional programming libraries called Cats and Doobie, and use them to write some interesting programs.

Chapter 8, Domain Specifc Languages, covers how Scala makes it possible to write powerful DSLs by providing a few interesting language features. Then, it'll cover a DSL that you'll very likely be using if you're going to work with Scala professionally.

Finally, you'll implement your own DSL.

What You Need for This Book

The minimum hardware requirements are as follows:

- Intel Core i3 processor
- 2 GB RAM
- An Internet connection

Please ensure you have the following software installed on your machine:

- Microsoft Windows 10/8/7 (64 bit)
- JDK 8
- IntelliJ + Scala plugin

Mac

- macOS 10.5 or higher (64-bit)
- JDK 8
- IntelliJ + Scala plugin

Linux

- Linux 64-bit
- KDE, GNOME, or Unity DE desktop
- JDK 8
- IntelliJ + Scala plugin

Conventions

In this book, you will find a number of text styles that distinguish between different kinds of information. Here are some examples of these styles and an explanation of their meaning.

Code words in text, database table names, folder names, filenames, file extensions, pathnames, dummy URLs, user input, and Twitter handles are shown as follows:

Here, we define an immutable value with the name name, which keeps the user's stdin.

The main method is an essential part of any Scala program.

A block of code is set as follows:

```
package com.packt.courseware
import scala.io.StdIn
object Chatbot1
{
   def main(args: Array[String]):Unit =  {
     // do something
   }
}
```

New terms and important words are shown in bold. Words that you see on the screen, for example, in menus or dialog boxes, appear in the text like this: " **Select Run sbt-test**."

Important new **programming terms** are shown in bold. *Conceptual terms* are shown in italics.

 Important additional details about a topic appear like this, as in a sidebar.

 Important notes, tips, and tricks appear like this.

Installation and Setup

Before we start this book, we'll install IntelliJ IDE.

Installing IntelliJ IDE

1. Visit https://www.jetbrains.com/idea/ in your browser.

2. Click on the **DOWNLOAD** button on the web page.

3. Choose your appropriate OS and, under **Community**, click on the **Download** option.

4. Follow the steps in the installer and that's it! Your IntelliJ IDE is ready.

Installing Scala plugin (make heading)

1. Open IntelliJ IDEA.
2. Go to `File Menu`.
3. In the file menu, select `Plugins`.
4. Click on `Browse repositories` button and enter `Scala`.
5. Select `Scala` plugin to install it.

Reader Feedback

Feedback from our readers is always welcome. Let us know what you think about this book—what you liked or disliked. Reader feedback is important for us as it helps us develop titles that you will really get the most out of.

To send us general feedback, simply e-mail `feedback@packtpub.com`, and mention the book's title in the subject of your message.

If there is a topic that you have expertise in and you are interested in either writing or contributing to a book, see our author guide at `www.packtpub.com/authors`.

Customer Support

Now that you are the proud owner of a Packt book, we have a number of things to help you to get the most from your purchase.

Downloading the Example Code

You can download the example code files from your account at `http://www.packtpub.com` for all the Packt Publishing books you have purchased. If you purchased this book elsewhere, you can visit `http://www.packtpub.com/support` and register to have the files e-mailed directly to you.

Errata

Although we have taken every care to ensure the accuracy of our content, mistakes do happen. If you find a mistake in one of our books—maybe a mistake in the text or the code—we would be grateful if you could report this to us. By doing so, you can save other readers from frustration and help us improve subsequent versions of this book. If you find any errata, please report them by visiting http://www.packtpub.com/submit-errata, selecting your book, clicking on the **Errata Submission Form** link, and entering the details of your errata. Once your errata are verified, your submission will be accepted and the errata will be uploaded to our website or added to any list of existing errata under the Errata section of that title.

To view the previously submitted errata, go to https://www.packtpub.com/books/content/support and enter the name of the book in the search field. The required information will appear under the **Errata** section.

Piracy

Piracy of copyrighted material on the Internet is an ongoing problem across all media. At Packt, we take the protection of our copyright and licenses very seriously. If you come across any illegal copies of our works in any form on the Internet, please provide us with the location address or website name immediately so that we can pursue a remedy.

Please contact us at copyright@packtpub.com with a link to the suspected pirated material.

We appreciate your help in protecting our authors and our ability to bring you valuable content.

Questions

If you have a problem with any aspect of this book, you can contact us at questions@packtpub.com, and we will do our best to address the problem.

Setting up the Development Environment

1

Before we start writing the various programs in this book, let's talk a little about the Scala language itself. Why is it necessary, and what has made Scala unique? What are the most important aspects of the language?

Scala was created in 2001 in EPFL (École Polytechnique Fédérale de Lausanne), by Martin Odersky. This is the same lab where Pascal language (widely used up to the end of the 1990s) was created.

Scala is an abbreviation for 'Scalable Language' — a language which can be scaled, that is, it allows you to write complex systems with gigantic amounts of functionality. As specified on Scala's home page: *"Scala combines object-oriented and functional programming in one concise, high-level language."*

> You can visit Scala's official home page here:
> `https://www.scala-lang.org/`

By the end of this chapter, you will be able to:

- Recognize the structure of a Scala project
- Identify the use of Scala's sbt tool (interactive build tool) for building and running your project
- Identify how to use the IDE
- Implement interactions with a simple chatbot

Scala is built on top of the JVM platform (the Scala program is compiled to use JVM bytecode).

Now, the language is used as one of the most preferred platforms in many areas, such as high-load soft-realtime applications, ad servers for data science toolkits.

Some characteristics of Scala are as follows:

- An advanced type system, which makes Scala superior (but at the same time, more complex) compared to most other industrial programming languages.
- Static typing, which allows you to write code in a safe way when errors are checked during compilation.

In this chapter, we will learn the basics of Scala, such as what the simple Scala program looks like and what a typical developer flow is. A significant part of development is interaction with tools—build tools, dependency extractors, IDEs, and so on, which form the tool ecosystem with the language. We will build a simple program using mainstream tools.

Simple Program

In this section, we will be covering the structure of a basic Scala program. We will be covering definitions such as packages, imports, and objects. We will also be looking into the main method of a Scala program.

Let's create the simplest possible program in Scala. We will implement a program which will print "Hello World" on the screen. The structure of this program is defined as follows:

```scala
package com.packt.courseware
import scala.io.StdIn
object Chatbot1
{
   def main(args: Array[String]):Unit = {
     // do something
   }
}
```

Definitions: Packages, Imports, and Objects

If you look at the preceding code, the first line is a package name. In our case, this is `com.packt.courseware`.

All compilation units are organized into packages. Packages can be nested, forming hierarchical namespaces for code objects.

When a compilation unit has no package declaration, it belongs to a so-called `'default'` package. Modules from a default package can't be imported from another package.

Usually, the source directory in a Scala project is organized in the same way as packages. This is not mandatory, but becomes a rule of thumb. Some tools (such as IDEs) use these conventions for default project settings.

Now we will look at `import` statements.

Object Definition

Here, we define the object `Chatbot1`.

If you are familiar with the traditional classes, since they are implemented in Java, you can look at the object of a class with one default instance, that is, an object is an implementation of the singleton pattern: on the JVM level, the object definition creates a class and one predefined instance of this class.

The main Method

Finally, the main method is an entry point for our program. It must accept an array of strings (command-line arguments) and return a unit.

Historically, the main method name is used in Scala. This is because the Java language is following the same tradition, which takes the name of an entry method from C, which take this from BCPL.

The method is defined as follows:

```
package com.packt.couserware
object X  { def f() = { … } }
```

Inside main

The main method is an essential part of any Scala program. The execution of a program first starts from the main method.

Let's look inside the main method:

```
def main(args: Array[String]): Unit = {
  val name = StdIn.readLine("Hi! What is your name?")
  println(s" $name, tell me something interesting, say 'bye' to end
the talk")
  var timeToBye = false  while (!timeToBye)
    timeToBye = StdIn.readLine(">") match {
      case "bye" => println("ok, bye")
                              true
      case  _       => println("interesting...")
                              false
    }
}
```

Here, we define an immutable value with the name name, which keeps the user's input from stdin. Scala is a statically typed language, and so the value is of type String.

As we can see, the type of the value is not explicitly written, but automatically inferred from its context.

At the next line, the value is printed using the "string interpolation" operator: In a string with a prefix of s, all occurrences of expressions inside ${} brackets in strings are replaced with values of these expressions, casted to strings. For simple identifiers, we can omit {} brackets, for example, in a string interpolation of s"x=$y", the value of y will be substituted instead with $y.

`var timeToBye` is a mutable variable with a `Boolean` type. Unlike values, mutable variables can be assigned more than once.

Looking forward at the loop, we can see that the program is trying to be a good listener and answer `interesting` to any message, except `bye`.

The result of the case statement is assigned to `timeToBye`, and is checked in the `while` loop condition

Scala, as a multiparadigm language, has both mutable and immutable variables. For nearly any task, we can choose more than one way of implementing this.

If guidelines exist, where should we use mutable variables and where should we use immutable variables?

Generally, reasoning about immutable variables is simpler. The usual heuristic is to use immutable values as much as possible, leaving mutable variables for performance-critical sections and state-check language constructs (such as while loops).

In our small example, we can eliminate the mutable flag by putting an expression for the loop exit condition inside `while`. The resulting code is smaller and better to read, but adding new functionality becomes harder. Yet there is one possibility — use the `recursive` function instead of the loop language construction.

Now let's add some functionality to our `chatbot`: when the user asks for the `time`, the `chatbot` should report the current time.

To do this, we must retrieve the current time using the Java API and display the output of the time using string interpolators.

For example, use the `now` method of `java.time.LocalTime`.

The code used to display this will be `println("time is ${java.time.LocalTime. now()}")`.

The following is the code for this functionality, but we will actually implement this after setting up the working environment we will be playing with:

```
package com.packt.courseware
package com.packt.courseware

import scala.io.StdIn

object Chatbot1 {

  def main(args: Array[String]): Unit = {
```

```
    val name = StdIn.readLine("Hi! What is your name?")
    println(s" $name, tell me something interesting, say 'bye' to end
the talk")
    var timeToBye = false
    while (!timeToBye)
        timeToBye = StdIn.readLine(">") match {
          case "bye" => println("ok, bye")
          true
          case "time" => println(s"time is ${java.time.LocalTime.
now()}")
          true
          case _ => println("interesting...")
          false
        }
}

}
```

Structure of a Scala Project

Let's look at our chatbot program in a complete runnable project. Let's navigate to
the /day1-lesson1/1-project directory in our code supplement.

The code is available on Github at the following link:
https://github.com/TrainingByPackt/
Professional-Scala

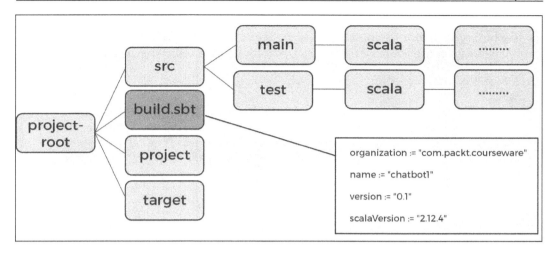

The preceding diagram is the typical directory structure of a Scala project. If you are familiar with the Java tools ecosystem, then you will notice the similarities between the maven project layout.

In src, we can see project sources (main and test). target is a place where output artifacts are created, whereas project is used as a place to internally build the project. We will cover all of these concepts later on.

```
organization := "com.packt.courseware"
name := "chatbot1"
version := "0.1-SNAPSHOT"
scalaVersion := "2.12.4"
```

The head of any project is its build.sbt file. It consists of the following code:

The text inside it is a plain Scala snippet.

organization, name, and version are instances of sbt.key. For this point of view, := is a binary operator defined on keys. In Scala, any method with two arguments can be used with the syntax of a binary operator. := is a valid method name.

build.sbt is interpreted by the sbt tool.

 sbt – The original intention for the name, when sbt was created by Mark Harrah, was 'Simple Build Tool'. Later on, the author decided to avoid such a decipherment, and kept it as it was. You can read about the details of sbt here: https://www.scala-sbt.org/1.x/docs/index.html.

Basic sbt Commands

We will now talk about the basic sbt commands.

sbt compile should compile the project and live somewhere in its target compiled Java classes.

sbt run executes the main function of the project. Therefore, we can try to interact with our chatbot:

```
rssh3:1-project rssh$ sbt run
[info] Loading global plugins from /Users/rssh/.sbt/0.13/plugins
[info] Set current project to chatbot1 (in build file:/Users/rssh/
work/packt/professional-scala/Lesson 1/1-project/)
[info] Running com.packt.courseware.Chatbot1
Hi! What is your name? Jon
  Jon, tell me something interesting, say 'bye' to end the talk

>qqq
interesting..
>ddd
interesting...
>bye
ok, bye
  [success] Total time: 19 s, completed Dec 1, 2017 7:18:42 AM
```

The output of the code is as follows:

sbt package prepares an output artifact. After running it, it will create file called target/chatbot1_2.12-0.1-SNAPSHOT.jar.

`chatbot1` is the name of our project; `0.1-SNAPSHOT` – version. `2.12` is the version of the Scala compiler.

Scala guarantees binary compatibility only within the scope of a minor version. If, for some reason, the project still uses `scala-2.11`, then it must use the library, which was created for `scala-2.11`. On the other hand, updating to the next compiler version can be a long process for projects with many dependencies. To allow the same library to exist in the repository with different `scalaVersions`, we need to have an appropriate suffix in the jar file.

`sbt publish-local` – publishes the artifact on to your local repository.

Now let's see our sample project and `sbt` tool.

Activity: Performing Basic Operations with sbt: Build, Run, Package

1. Install sbt on your computer, if not installed beforehand.
2. Start the `sbt` console by typing `sbt console` in the root directory of the `1-project` (where `build.sbt` is situated).
3. Compile the code by typing the `compile` command into the `sbt` console.
4. Run the program by typing the `sbt run` command into the `sbt` console.
5. When running this, say `bye` to the bot and return to the console.
6. Package the program by typing `package` into the `sbt` console.

IDE

Another part of the developer toolbox is an IDE tool (Integrated Development Environment). For our book, we will use Intellij IDEA community edition with the Scala plugin. This is not the only option: other alternatives are scala-ide, based on IBM Eclipse and Ensime (`http://ensime.github.io/`), which brings IDE features to any programmable text editors, from vi to emacs.

All tools support importing the project layout from `build.sbt`.

Activity: Loading and Running a Sample Project in the IDE

1. Import our project:

   ° Go to `File` -> `Import` -> navigate to `build.sbt`

2. Open the program in IDE:

   ° Start IDEA

   ° Press `Open`

   ° Select `day1-lesson1/1-project/build.sbt`

3. In the dialog window, which asks whether to open it as a file or as a project, select `project`.

4. On the left part of the project's structure, unfold `src` entry.

5. Click on `main`.

6. Ensure that you can see `main`, as specified in the code.

7. Ensure that project can be compiled and run via the `sbt` console.

For running our project from the IDE, we should edit the project's configuration (Menu: `Build/Edit configuration` or `Run/Edit` configuration, depending on which version of IDEA you are using).

Running the Project from IDE:

1. Select `Run/Edit Configuration`.

2. Select `Application`.

3. Set the application's name. In our case, use `Chatbot1`.

4. Set the name of the `Main` class. In our case, it must be `com.packt.courseware.Chatbot1`.

5. Actually run the application: select Run, then Chatbot1 from the dropdown menu.

REPL

Another tool that we will frequently use is REPL (Read Eval Print Loop). It is often used for quickly evaluating Scala expressions.

From `sbt`, we can enter REPL mode with the help of the `sbt console` command. Let's try some simple expressions.

Now, we'll look at how to evaluate expressions. Follow these steps to do so:

1. Open the `sbt` tool.

2. Open `REPL` by typing the following command:

   ```
   sbt console
   ```

3. Type the following expressions and press *Enter*:

   - `2 + 2`
   - `"2" + 2`
   - `2 + "2"`
   - `(1 to 8).sum`
   - `java.time.LocalTime.now()`

Please note that we can have an interactive Scala `playboard` inside IDE by creating a special file type: a Scala Worksheet. It's useful, but is mainly for demonstration purposes.

Obtaining the Time Request from Our Chatbot Program

For now, let's return to our task: modifying the `chatbot` program so that it replies with the current time, as requested by the use of `time`. Let's learn how to do this:

Steps for Completion

1. Check for `time` to match the statement:

   ```
   case "time" =>
   ```

2. Retrieve the current time using the Java API. Use the `now` method of `java.time.LocalTime`:

   ```
   java.time.LocalTime.now()
   ```

3. Display the output of the time using string interpolators, as follows:

   ```
   println("time is ${java.time.LocalTime.now()}")
   ```

The `main` method will look like this:

```
def main(args: Array[String]): Unit = {
    val name = StdIn.readLine("Hi! What is your name?")
    println(s" $name, tell me something interesting, say 'bay' to end
the talk")
    var timeToBye = false
```

```
        while (!timeToBye)
            timeToBye = StdIn.readLine(">") match {
                case "bye" => println("ok, bye")
                true
                case "time" => println(s"time is ${java.time.LocalTime.
now()}")
                true
                case _ => println("interesting...")
                false
            }
}
```

After we prepare and package our artifacts, we need to run them as well.

In this book, we will use the running system from unpackaged sources via sbt (as in the early days of Ruby applications), assuming that sources and sbt tools are accessible from the production environment. Using this, we can use build tool commands for sources such as sbt run. In real life, packaging for production is a bit more complex.

Popular methods for doing this are as follows:

- Preparing a fat jar (which includes all dependencies). An sbt plugin for this exists, which can be found at the following link: https://github.com/sbt/ sbt-assembly.

- Preparing a native system package (which includes jars, dependencies, custom layouts, and so on). There is also an sbt plugin to create native system packages, which can be found at the following link: https:// github.com/sbt/sbt-native-packager.

Base Syntax

Now that we can use REPL, let's understand the base Scala syntax. For now, it's not necessary to learn it in detail, but let's get familiar with it by using an example.

For a formal, detailed description, refer to the SLS: Scala Language Specification here: http://scala-lang.org/files/archive/ spec/2.12/.

Base Syntax for Definitions

Scala compilation unit – This is a set of definitions inside an entity (template-entity), which can be an object, a class, or a trait. We will speak about the Object-Oriented part of the Scala language in detail later. Now, let's look at the basic syntax. Let's define some classes in REPL:

```
> class X {  def f():Int = 1 }
> Class X defined  // answer in REPL
```

Definitions inside the entity can be nested entities, functions, or values:

```
> def f():Int = 1
```

Here, the function f is defined, returning 1. We will talk about this function in detail in *Chapter 3*, *Functions*. Now, let's stay on the top-level view:

```
> val x = 1
```

Here, the value x is defined with value 1:

```
> var y = 2
```

Here, the mutable variable y is defined with value 2.

Other high-level entities include objects and traits. We can create objects by writing object or trait definitions:

```
>  object O {  def f():Int =1  }
>  trait O {  def f():Int =1  }
```

We will talk about classes, objects, and traits in the next chapter.

Now, let's look at defining an object in REPL with the name ZeroPoint.

Steps for Completion:

1. Open REPL by typing the following command in sbt:
    ```
    sbt console
    ```

2. Type in the following commands in REPL:
    ```
    >  object ZeroPoint {
    >     val x:Int = 0
    >     val y:Int = 0
    > }
    ```

Base Syntax for Expressions

Scala is an expression-based language, which means that everything is an expression (in the right-hand side of function and value/variable definitions).

Some of the base expressions are:

- Primitive expression: Constant or value/variable name.
- Function calls: These can be:
  - Usual function calls `f(x, y)`.
  - Operator call syntax:
  - binary: `x + y`.

 Any method with an argument can be used as a binary operator. A set of predefined binary operators are similar to Java:

- unary: `!x`
- Constructors: `new x` creates an instance of class `x`.
- Assignments to mutable variables:
  - `y = 3`: Assigns a value of `3` to `y`.
  - `x = 3`: This is a compiler error, and a value can't be assigned.
- Block:

  ```
  { A; B }
  ```

  The value of a block expression is the last expression. Note that `;` can be omitted if `A` and `B` are situated on different lines. The syntax for this is shown as follows:

  ```
  {
    A
    B
  }
  ```

The preceding syntax will have the same output as `{ A; B }`.

- Control structures
  - `if` statement:

    ```
    >  if (1 == 1)  "A"  else "B"
    - let's eval one in REPL
    ```

○ match/case expressions:

```
>  x match {
     case "Jon"  =>  doSomethingSpecialForJon()
     case "Joe" =>   doSomethingSpecialForJoe()
     case     _   => doForAll()
   }
```

○ Loops:

○ while/do

```
var i=0
 var s=0
 while(i < 10) {
     s = s+i
     i = i +1
 }
```

○ Do/while

○ Foreach, for

Shortcuts for height-order functions will be described in detail in, *Chapter 4, Scala Collections*.

We'll look at defining a main function which prints something onscreen and calls the main function.

1. You should have already opened `project1`. If you haven't, import it into the IDE.

2. Insert the new method inside the object definition.

3. Insert call at the `main` method.

The full method should look something like this:

```
object Chatbot1 {

  def printHello():Unit = {
     println("Hello")
  }

  def main(args: Array[String]): Unit = {
    printHello()
    … // unchanged code here
  }

}
```

Unit Testing

In any program which is bigger than arithmetic operations, programmers should make themselves comfortable when it is possible to ensure that new changes are not breaking old functionalities.

The most common technique for this is unit testing, which is where the programmer tests the functionality of the code in parallel with its development by creating a test code which will verify that the code really satisfies their requirements.

The theme of this section will be introducing tools for unit testing in Scala.

Adding a Test to Our Project

Let's add tests to our small program. We'll import `<for-students/lesson1/2-project>` in our IDE.

This is the directory schema of a Scala project. For adding tests, we should do the following:

- Add test dependencies to `build.sbt`
- Write tests in the source test directory

For adding dependency, let's add the following line to our `build.sbt`:

```
libraryDependencies += "org.scalatest" %% "scalatest" % "3.0.4" %
"test"
```

It's an expression in Scala DSL (domain-specific language), which means that we should add `scalatest` to our set of library dependencies. Operators `%%` and `%` are used for forming the name and classifier for published artifacts. You can refer to the `sbt` documentation for more detail: `http://www.scala-sbt.org/1.x/docs/Library-Dependencies.html`.

Before compilation, `sbt` will download `scalatest` from a publicly available repository (Maven central), and when running tests, it will add `scalatest` to the classpath.

We will now run `sbt` tests from the command line.

1. In the command-line environment, navigate to the root of the project and select the following test:

   ```
   Lesson 1/2-project
   ```

2. If you are using a Unix/Linux machine and your code is situated in `courses/`
   `pactscala` of your home `directory`, then run the following command:

   ```
   > cd  ~/courses/packscala/Lesson 1/2-project
   ```

3. Run the following command :

   ```
   > sbt test
   ```

4. You will get the expected output, which will include the following strings:

   ```
   [info] ExampleSpec:
   [info] - example test should pass
   [info] StepTest:
   [info] - step of unparded word must be interesting
   ```

We will now see how to run `sbt` tests from IDEA IDE.

We'll now run sbt Tests from IDEA IDE.

1. Open the project in the IDE.

2. Navigate to **Run/Edit Configurations:**

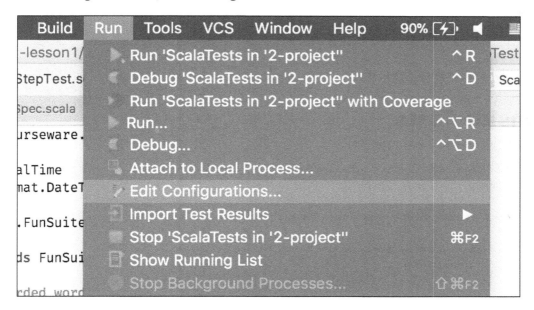

3. Choose sbt test as the configuration.

  ○ Check the checkbox **Use sbt:**

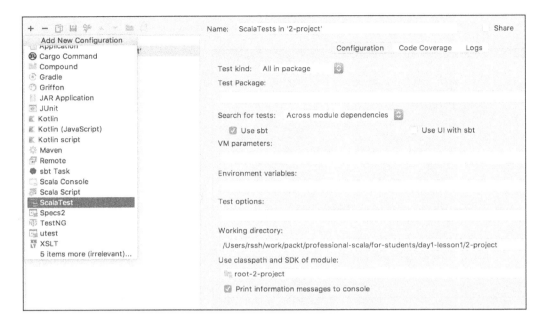

4. Select **Run sbt-test**.

Inside Tests

Now let's look at a simple test:

```
package com.packt.courseware.l1
import org.scalatest.FunSuite

class ExampleSpec extends FunSuite {

  test("example test  should pass") {
     assert(1==1)
  }

}
```

Here, we define a class which is inherited from scalatest FunSuite.

The test expression is called. When the `FunSuite` class is initialized and added to a set of tests, the test with `name example test should pass` and assert an expression as an argument. For now, this looks like magic, but we will show you how to build such DSLs in the next chapter.

Let's run our test with the help of `sbt`:

```
sbt test
```

This command will run all tests and evaluate the test expression.

Now, we'll add another test.

1. Add one more test to the same file: `src/test/scala/com/packt/courseware/l1/ExampleSpec.scala` in `2-project`

2. We write one `trivial` test, which asserts the `false` expression:

```
test("trivial")  {
        assert(false)
   }
```

3. Run the test and look at error reporting.

4. Invert the expression in assert so that the test passes:

```
test("trivial")  {
        assert(true)
   }
```

5. Run the `sbt` test again to ensure that all of the tests pass.

Running Tests for Chatbot

Remember that, when writing `chatbot`, we want to test one functionality. Our original program only has one function (`main`), which contains all of the logic and can't be split into testable parts.

Let's look at Version 2.

 Please import `Lesson 1/2-project` into your IDE.

```scala
package com.packt.courseware.l1

import java.time.LocalTime
import java.time.format.DateTimeFormatter
import scala.io.StdIn

case class LineProcessResult(answer:String,timeToBye:Boolean)

object Chatbot2 {

  def main(args: Array[String]): Unit = {
    val name = StdIn.readLine("Hi! What is your name? ")
    println(s" $name, tell me something interesting, say 'bye' to end
the talk")

    var c = LineProcessResult("",false)
    while(!c.timeToBye){
      c = step(StdIn.readLine(">"))
      println(c.answer)
    }

  }

  def step(input:String): LineProcessResult = {
    input match {
      case "bye" => LineProcessResult("ok, bye", true)
      case "time" => LineProcessResult(LocalTime.now().
format(DateTimeFormatter.ofPattern("HH:mm:ss")),false)
      case _ => LineProcessResult("interesting...", false)
    }
  }

}
```

Here, we see some new constructs:

LineProcessingResult is a case class, where the result of processing one of the lines (that is, the chatbot answer and quit flag) is stored.

What is the word case before class?

case classes can participate in pattern matching (while we call one case) and are usually used for data objects. We will look at case classes during the next chapter. It is important to see that an instance of case classes can be created with the LineProcessingResult(x,y) syntax (that is, without new) and an argument to case class constructors (answers and timeToBye), which automatically become instance variables of the case class.

The functionality of processing one line is encapsulated in the step method, which we can test.

Step receives input from the method argument, not from System.in, therefore making it easier to test. In the case of directly testing the main method, we will need to substitute System.in before test and return one back after the test is finished.

Ok, let's focus on the first test:

```
package com.packt.courseware.l1

import org.scalatest.FunSuite

class StepTestSpec extends FunSuite {

  test("step of unparded word must be interesting") {
    val r = Chatbot2.step("qqqq")
    assert(! r.timeToBye)
    assert(r.answer == "interesting...")
  }

}
```

Writing the second test in the same manner will be an easy task. We will look at this in the following exercise.

Now, let's add the second test, which checks bye.

1. Add a second test to the StepTestSpec class in our project:

    ```
    test("after bye, timeToBye should be set to true")
    {

    }
    ```

2. In this test:

   ° Call the step function with `bye` as a parameter:

```
val r = Chatbot2.step("bye")
```

   ° Check that after this call that `timeToQuit` in the returned class is set to `true`:

```
assert(! r.timeToBye)
```

3. The whole code should be as follows:

```
test("after bye, timeToBye should be set to true") {
  val r = Chatbot2.step("bye")
assert(! r.timeToBye)
```

4. Run `sbt test`.

A more complex task would be to write a test for the time query.

Please note that we can't run the test with the concrete time value, but at least we can be sure that the bot answer can't be parsed back to the time form.

So, what can we do to check the line answer and try to transform it back to time? The solution is provided in the following code:

```
test("local time must be parser") {
  val r = Chatbot2.step("time")
  val formatter = DateTimeFormatter.ofPattern("HH:mm:ss")
  val t = LocalTime.parse(r.answer,formatter)
  // assertion is not necessary
}
```

Note that assertion is not necessary. If time does not satisfy the given format, then an exception will be thrown.

It is a good practice to separate functional and effects time for testing. To do this, we will need to substitute the provider of the system time via own.

This will be the first practical task in the next chapter.

Now, let's add the date command to our chatbot program.

1. Add the following code to the match statement so that it checks for the `date` command, which should output the local date in `DD:MM:YYYY` format:

```
case "date" => LineProcessResult(LocalDate.now().
format(DateTimeFormatter.ofPattern("dd:YYYY-MM")),false)
```

2. Add a test case for this function.

3. The resulting code will be as follows:

```
test("local date must be parser") {
  val r = Chatbot2.step("date")
  val formatter = DateTimeFormatter.ofPattern("dd:MM-YYYY")
  val t = LocalDate.parse(r.answer,formatter)
  // assertion is not necessary
}
```

Summary

We have reached the end of the chapter. In this chapter, we learned various aspects of setting up the development environment. We covered the structure of a Scala project, and we identified the use of sbt for building and running projects. We covered REPL, which is a command-line interface for running Scala code. We also covered how to develop and run code over the IDEA IDE. Finally, we implemented interactions with our simple chatbot application.

In the next chapter, we will cover the structure of a Scala program and dive deep into the object-oriented properties in Scala, such as like classes, objects, and traits. We will also cover the syntax for calling functions and various parameter-passing models.

2
Basic Language Features

In the previous chapter, we learned the various aspects of setting up the development environment wherein we covered the structure of a Scala project and identified the use of `sbt` for building and running projects. We covered REPL, which is a command-line interface for running Scala code, and how to develop and run code over the IDEA IDE. Finally, we implemented interactions with our simple `chatbot` application.

In this chapter, we will explore the so-called 'OO' part of Scala, which allows us to build constructions similar to analogs in any mainstream language, such as Java or C++. The object-oriented part of Scala will cover classes and objects, traits, pattern matching, case class, and so on. Finally, we will implement the object-oriented concepts that we learn to our chatbot application.

Looking at the history of programming paradigms, we will notice that the first generation of high-level programming languages (Fortran, C, Pascal) were procedure oriented, without OO or FP facilities. Then, OO become a hot topic in programming languages in the 1980s.

By the end of this chapter, you will be able to do the following:

- Identify the structure of non-trivial Scala programs
- Identify how to use main object-oriented facilities: objects, classes, and traits
- Recognize the details of function call syntax and parameter-passing modes

Objects, Classes, and Traits

Scala is a multiparadigm language, which unites functional and OO programming. Now, we will explore Scala's traditional object-oriented programming facilities: object, classes, and traits.

These facilities are similar in the sense that each one contains some sets of data and methods, but they are different regarding life cycle and instance management:

- Objects are used when we need a type with one instance (such as singletons)
- Classes are used when we need to have many instances, which can be created with the help of the new operator
- Traits are used for mix-ins into other classes

Note that it is not worth navigating through code, as this is exposed in examples.

Object

We have seen an object in the previous chapter. Let's scroll through our codebase and open the file named `Main` in `Lesson 2/3-project`:

```scala
object Chatbot3 {

 val effects = DefaultEffects

 def main(args: Array[String]): Unit = {

   ….

 }

   def createInitMode() = (Bye or CurrentDate or CurrentTime) otherwise
InterestingIgnore
}
```

It's just a set of definitions, grouped into one object, which is available statically. That is, the implementation of a singleton pattern: we only have one instance of an object of a given type.

Here, we can see the definition of the value (`val effects`) and main functions. The syntax is more-or-less visible. One non-obvious thing is that the `val` and `var` definitions that are represented are not plain field, but internal field and pairs of functions: the `getter` and `setter` functions for `var-s`. This allows overriding `def-s` by `val-s`.

Note that the name in the object definition is a name of an object, not a name of the type. The type of the object, `Chatbot3`, can be accessed as `Chatbot3.type`.

Let's define the object and call a method. We will also try to assign the object to a variable.

 You should have `project-3` opened in IDEA.

1. Navigate to the project structure and find the `com.packt.courseware.13` package.

2. Right-click and select `create class` in the context menu.

3. Enter `ExampleObject` in the name field and choose `object` in the kind field of the form.

4. IDEA will generate the file in the object.

5. Insert the following in the object definition:

```
def hello(): Unit = {
    println("hello")
  }
- navigate to main object
 Insert before start of main method:
  val example = ExampleObject
 Insert at the beginning of the main method:
   example.hello()
```

Classes

Classes form the next step in abstractions. Here is an example of a class definition:

```
package com.packt.courseware.14

import math._

class PolarPoint(phi:Double, radius:Double) extends Point2D
{
 require(phi >= - Pi && phi < Pi )
 require(radius >= 0)

 def this(phi:Double) = this(phi,1.0)

 override def length = radius

 def x: Double = radius*cos(phi)
```

```
    def y: Double = radius*sin(phi)

    def * (x:Double) = PolarPoint(phi,radius*x)
}
```

Here is a class with parameters (phi, radius) specified in the class definition. Statements outside the class methods (such as require statements) constitute the body of a primary constructor.

The next definition is a secondary constructor, which must call the primary constructor at the first statement.

We can create an object instance using the new operator:

```
val p = new PolarPoint(0)
```

By default, member access modifiers are public, so once we have created an object, we can use its methods. Of course, it is possible to define the method as protected or private.

Sometimes, we want to have constructor parameters available in the role of class members. A special syntax for this exists:

```
case class PolarPoint(val phi:Double, val radius:Double) extends
Point2D
```

If we write val as a modifier of the constructor argument (phi), then phi becomes a member of the class and will be available as a field.

If you browse the source code of a typical Scala project, you will notice that an object with the same name as a class is often defined along with the class definition. Such objects are called companion objects of a class:

```
object PolarPoint
{

  def apply(phi:Double, r:Double) = new PolarPoint(phi,r)

}
```

This is a typical place for utility functions, which in the Java world are usually represented by static methods.

Method names also exist, which allow you to use special syntax sugar on the call side. We will tell you about all of these methods a bit later. We will talk about the `apply` method now.

When a method is named `apply`, it can be called via functional call braces (for example, x(y) is the same as x.apply(y), if apply is defined in x).

Conventionally, the `apply` method in the companion object is often used for instance creation to allow the syntax without the `new` operator. So, in our example, `PolarPoint(3.0,5.0)` will be demangled to `PolarPoint.apply(3.0,5.0)`.

Now, let's define a case class, CartesianPoint, with the method length.

1. Ensure that the `Lesson 2/4-project` project is open in IDE.
2. Create a new Scala class with the name `CartesianPoint`.
3. The code should be something like this:

```
case class CartesianPoint(x:Double, y:Double) extends Point2D {

    override def length(): Double = x*x + y*y

}
```

Equality and Case Classes

In general, two flavors of equality exist:

*   **Extensional**, where two objects are equal when all external properties are equal.
    *   In JVM, a user can override equals and `hashCode` methods of an object to achieve such a behavior.
    *   In a Scala expression, x == y is a shortcut of x.equals(y) if x is a reference type (for example, a class or object).
*   **Intentional** (or reference), where two objects with the same properties can be different because they had been created in a different time and context.
    *   In JVM, this is the comparison of references; (x == y) in Java and (x eq y) in Scala.

Looking at our `PolarPoint`, it looks as though if we want `PolarPoint(0,1)` to be equal `PolarPoint(0,1)`, then we must override `equals` and `hashCode`.

The Scala language provides a flavor of classes, which will do this work (and some others) automatically.

Let's see the `case` classes:

```
case class PolarPoint(phi:Double, radius:Double) extends Point2D
```

When we mark a class as a case class, the Scala compiler will generate the following:

- `equals` and `hashCode` methods, which will compare classes by components
- A `toString` method which will output components
- A `copy` method, which will allow you to create a copy of the class, with some of the fields changed:

```
val p1 = PolarPoint(Pi,1)
val p2 = p1.copy(phi=1)
```

- All parameter constructors will become class values (therefore, we do not need to write `val`)
- The companion object of a class with the apply method (for constructor shortcuts) and `unapply` method (for deconstruction in case patterns)

Now, we'll look at illustrating the differences between value and reference equality.

1. In `test/com.packt.courseware.14`, create a worksheet.

 To create a worksheet, navigate to package, and right-click and choose create a Scala worksheet from the drop-down menu.

2. Define a non-case class with fields in this file after import:

```
class NCPoint(val x:Int, val y:Int)
val ncp1 = new NCPoint(1,1)
val ncp2 = new NCPoint(1,1)

ncp1 == ncp2
ncp1 eq ncp2
```

 Notice that the results are `false`.

3. Define the case class with the same fields:

```
case class CPoint(x:Int, y:Int)
```

4. Write a similar test. Note the differences:

```
val cp1 = CPoint(1,1)
val cp2 = CPoint(1,1)

cp1 == cp2
cp1 eq cp2
```

Pattern Matching

Pattern matching is a construction that was first introduced into the ML language family near 1972 (another similar technique can also be viewed as a pattern-matching predecessor, and this was in REFAL language in 1968). After Scala, most new mainstream programming languages (such as Rust and Swift) also started to include pattern-matching constructs.

Let's look at pattern-matching usage:

```
val p = PolarPoint(0,1)
 val r = p match {
 case PolarPoint(_,0) => "zero"
 case x: PolarPoint if (x.radius == 1) => s"r=1, phi=${x.phi}"
 case v@PolarPoint(x,y) => s"(x=${x},y=${y})"
 case _ => "not polar point"
 }
```

On the second line, we see a match/case expression; we match p against the sequence of case-e clauses. Each case clause contains a pattern and body, which is evaluated if the matched expression satisfies the appropriative pattern.

In this example, the first case pattern will match any point with a radius of 0, that is, _ match any.

Second–This will satisfy any `PolarPoint` with a radius of one, as specified in the optional pattern condition. Note that the new value (x) is introduced into the body context.

Third – This will match any point; bind x and y to `phi` and the `radius` accordingly, and v to the pattern (v is the same as the original matched pattern, but with the correct type).

The final case expression is a `default` case, which matches any value of p.

Note that the patterns can be nested.

As we can see, case classes can participate in case expression and provide a method for pushing matched values into the body's content (which is deconstructed).

Now, it's time to use match/case statements.

1. Create a class file in the test sources of the current project with the name `Person`.

2. Create a case class called `Person` with the members `firstName` and `lastName`:

    ```
    case class Person(firstName:String,lastName:String)
    ```

3. Create a companion object and add a method which accepts `person` and returns `String`:

    ```
    def classify(p:Person): String = {
     // insert match code here .
     ???
    }
    ```

4. Create a `case` statement, which will print:

    ○   "`A`" if the person's first name is "`Joe`"

    ○   "`B`" if the person does not satisfy other cases

    ○   "`C`" if the `lastName` starts in lowercase

5. Create a test-case for this method:

    ```
    class PersonTest extends FunSuite {

     test("Persin(Joe,_) should return A") {
     assert( Person.classify(Person("Joe","X")) == "A" )
     }
    }
    ```

Traits

Traits are used for grouping methods and values which can be used in other classes. The functionality of traits is mixed into other traits and classes, which in other languages are appropriative constructions called `mixins`. In Java 8, interfaces are something similar to traits, since it is possible to define default implementations. This isn't entirely accurate, though, because Java's default method can't fully participate in inheritance.

Let's look at the following code:

```
trait Point2D {

  def x: Double
  def y: Double

  def length():Double = x*x + y*y

}
```

Here is a trait, which can be extended by the `PolarPoint` class, or with the `CartesianPoint` with the next definition:

```
case class CartesianPoint(x:Double, y:Double) extends Point2D
```

Instances of traits cannot be created, but it is possible to create anonymous classes extending the trait:

```
val p = new Point2D {
  override def x: Double = 1
override def y: Double = 0
}
assert(p.length() == 1)
```

Here is an example of a trait:

```
trait A {
  def f = "f.A"
}

trait B {
  def f = "f.B"

  def g = "g.B"
}


trait C extends A with B {
  override def f = "f.C" // won't compile without override.
}
```

As we can see, the conflicting method must be overridden:

Yet one puzzle:

```
trait D1 extends B1 with C
{
 override def g = super.g
}

trait D2 extends C with B1
{
 override def g = super.g
}
```

The result of D1.g will be g.B, and D2.g will be g.C. This is because traits are linearized into sequence, where each trait overrides methods from the previous one.

Now, let's try to represent the diamond in a trait hierarchy.

Create the following entities:

Component – A base class with the description() method, which outputs the description of a component.

Transmitter – A component which generates a signal and has a method called generateParams.

Receiver – A component which accepts a signal and has a method called receiveParams.

Radio – A Transmitter and Receiver. Write a set of traits, where A is modelled as inheritance.

The answer to this should be as follows:

```
trait Component
{
 def description(): String
}

trait Transmitter extends Component
{
 def generateParams(): String
}

trait Receiver extends Component
{
 def receiverParame(): String
}
trait Radio extends Transmitter with Receiver
```

Self-Types

In Scale-trait, you can sometimes see the self-types annotation, for example:

 For full code, refer to `Code Snippets/Lesson 2.scala` file.

```scala
trait Drink
{
 def baseSubstation: String
 def flavour: String
 def description: String
}


trait VanillaFlavour
{
 thisFlavour: Drink =>

 def flavour = "vanilla"
 override def description: String = s"Vanilla ${baseSubstation}"
}

trait SpecieFlavour
{
 thisFlavour: Drink =>

 override def description: String = s"${baseSubstation} with ${flavour}"
}

trait Tee
{
   thisTee: Drink =>

   override def baseSubstation: String = "tee"

   override def description: String = "tee"


     def withSpecies: Boolean = (flavour != "vanilla")
}
```

Here, we see the `identifier` `=>` {typeName} prefix, which is usually a self-type annotation.

If the type is specified, that trait can only be mixed-in to this type. For example, `VanillaTrait` can only be mixed in with Drink. If we try to mix this with another object, we will receive an error.

 If `Flavor` is not extended from `Drink`, but has access to `Drink` methods such as looks, as in `Flavor`, we situate it inside Drink.

Also, self-annotation can be used without specifying a type. This can be useful for nested traits when we want to call "this" of an enclosing trait:

```
trait Out
{

 thisOut =>

 trait Internal
 {
   def f(): String = thisOut.g()
   def g(): String = .
   }

   def g(): String = ….
}
```

Sometimes, we can see the organization of some big classes as a set of traits, grouped around one 'base'. We can visualize this as 'Cake', which consists of the 'Pieces:' self-annotated trait. We can change one piece to another by changing the mix-in traits. Such an organization of code is named the 'Cake pattern'. Note that using the Cake pattern is often controversial, because it's relative easy to create a 'God object'. Also note that the refactor class hierarchy with the cake-pattern inside is harder to implement.

Now, let's explore annotations.

1. Create an instance of Drink with Tee with `VanillaFlavour` which refers to `description`:

```
val tee = new Drink with Tee with VanillaFlavour
val tee1 = new Drink with VanillaFlavour with Tee
tee.description
tee1.description
```

2. Try to override the description in the Tee class:

   Uncomment Tee: def description = plain tee in the Drinks file.

   Check if any error message arises.

3. Create the third object, derived from Drink with Tee and VanillaFlavour with an overloaded description:

```
val tee2 = new Drink with Tee with VanillaFlavour {
  override def description: String =
    "plain vanilla tee"
}
```

Also note that special syntax for methods exists, which must be 'mixed' after the overriding method, for example:

 For full code, refer to Code Snippets/Lesson 2.scala file.

```
trait Operation
{

  def doOperation(): Unit

}

trait PrintOperation
{
  this: Operation =>

  def doOperation():Unit = Console.println("A")
}

trait LoggedOperation extends Operation
{
  this: Operation =>

  abstract override def doOperation():Unit = {
    Console.print("start")
    super.doOperation()
    Console.print("end")
  }
}
```

Here, we see that the methods marked as `abstract override` can call `super` methods, which are actually defined in traits, not in this base class. This is a relatively rare technique.

Special Classes

There are a few classes with special syntax, which play a significant role in the Scala type system. We will cover this in detail later, but now let's just enumerate some:

- **Functions**: In Scala, this can be coded as `A => B`
- **Tuples**: In Scala, this can be coded as `(A,B)`, `(A,B,C)` ... and so on, which is a syntax sugar for `Tuple2[A,B]`, `Tuple3[A,B,C]`, and so on

OO in Our Chatbot

Now that you know the theoretical basics, let's look at these facilities and how they are used in our program. Let's open `Lesson 2/3-project` in our IDE and extend our chatbot, which was developed in the previous chapter.

Decoupling Logic and Environment

To do this, we must decouple the environment and logic, and integrate only one in the `main` method.

Let's open the `EffectsProvider` class:

 For full code, refer to `Code Snippets/Lesson 2.scala` file.

```
trait EffectsProvider extends TimeProvider {

  def input: UserInput

  def output: UserOutput

}

object DefaultEffects extends EffectsProvider
{
  override def input: UserInput = ConsoleInput

  override def output: UserOutput = ConsoleOutput
```

```scala
  override def currentTime(): LocalTime = LocalTime.now()

  override def currentDate(): LocalDate = LocalDate.now()
}
```

Here, we encapsulate all of the effects into our traits, which can have different implementations.

For example, let's look at `UserOutput`:

For full code, refer to `Code Snippets/Lesson 2.scala` file.

```scala
trait UserOutput {

  def write(message: String): Unit

  def writeln(message: String): Unit = {
   write(message)
   write("\n")
  }

}



object ConsoleOutput extends UserOutput
{

  def write(message: String): Unit = {
   Console.print(message)
  }
}
```

Here, we can see the trait and object, which implement the current trait. This way, when we need to accept commands that are not from standard input, but from the chatbot API or from Twitter, we only need to change the implementation of the `UserOutput`/`ConsoleOutput` interfaces.

It's now time to implement `ConsoleOutput` and `DefaultTimeProvider`.

Replace `???` in main with the appropriative constructor.

These steps for implementing `ConsoleOutput` and `DefaultTimeProvider` are as follows:

1. Ensure that `Lesson 2/3-project` is open in IDE.

2. In the `UserOutput` file, find the `ConsoleOutput` file and change `???` to the body of the `write` method. The resulting method should look like this:

```
object ConsoleOutput extends UserOutput
{

 def write(message: String): Unit = {
  Console.print(message)
  }
}
```

3. In the `TimeProvider` file, add the `DefaultTimeProvide` object which extends from `TimeProvider` and implements the `currentTime` and `currentDate` functions. The resulting code should look like this:

```
object DefaultTimeProvider extends TimeProvider {

  override def currentTime(): LocalTime = LocalTime.now()

  override def currentDate(): LocalDate = LocalDate.now()

}
```

Sealed Traits and Algebraic Datatypes

Let's deal with the second issue — let's encapsulate the logic of chatbot modes into the trait, which will only deal with logic and nothing else. Look at the following definition:

```
trait ChatbotMode {

  def process(message: String, effects: EffectsProvider):
LineStepResult

  def or(other: ChatbotMode): ChatbotMode = Or(this,other)

  def otherwise(other: ChatbotMode): ChatbotMode =
Otherwise(this,other)
}
```

For now, let's ignore or and otherwise combinators and look at the process method. It accepts input messages and effects and returns the processing result, which can be a failure or message sent to a user with the next state of the mode:

```
sealed trait LineStepResult

case class Processed(
  answer:String,
  nextMode: ChatbotMode,
 endOfDialog:Boolean) extends LineStepResult

case object Failed extends LineStepResult
```

Here, we can see a new modifier: sealed.

When a trait (or class) is sealed, it can only be extended in the same file, where it is defined. Due to this, you can be sure that, in your family of classes, nobody will be able to add a new class to somewhere in your project. If you do use case analysis with the help of the match/case expression, a compiler can do exhaustive checking: all of the variants are present.

Constructions from a family of case classes/objects, extended from a sealed trait, is often named an Algebraic Data Type (ADT).

This term comes to us from the HOPE language (1972, Edinburg University), where all types can be created from an initial set of types with the help of algebraic operations: among them was a named product (which looks like a case class in Scala) and distinct union (modeled by the sealed trait with subtyping).

Using ADT in domain modeling is rewarding because we can do evident case analysis for the domain model and have no weak abstraction; we can implement various designs which can be added to our model in the future.

Returning to our ChatbotMode.

On bye, we must exit the program.

This is easy — just define the appropriative object:

```
object Bye extends ChatbotMode {
  override def process(message: String, effects: EffectsProvider):
LineStepResult =
    if (message=="bye") {
     Processed("bye",this,true)
    } else Failed
  }
```

Now, we'll look at creating the same modes for the `CurrentTime` query.

 The code for this exercise can be found in `Lesson 2/3-project`.

1. Create a new file in the `CurrentTime` modes package.
2. Add one to the chain of modes in `Main` (for example, the Modify definition of `createInitMode`).
3. Make sure that `test`, which checks the time functionality, is passed.

The next step is to make a bigger mode from a few simpler modes. Let's look at the mode, which extends two modes and can select a mode which is able to process incoming messages:

```
case class Or(frs: ChatbotMode, snd: ChatbotMode) extends ChatbotMode
{
 override def process(message: String, effects: EffectsProvider):
LineStepResult =
  {
    frs.process(message, effects) match {
     case Processed(answer,nextMode,endOfDialog) => Processed(answer,
Or(nextMode,snd),endOfDialog)
      case Failed => snd.process(message,effects) match {
       case Processed(answer,nextMode,endOfDialog) => Processed(answer,
Or(nextMode,frs),endOfDialog)
        case Failed => Failed
      }
    }
  }

}
```

Here, if `frs` can process a message, then the result of processing this is returned. It will contain an answer. `NextMode` (which will accept the next sequence) is the same or with `nextMode` from `frs`, processing the result and `snd`.

If `frs` can't answer this, then we try `snd`. If `snd`'s processing is successful, then, in the next dialog step, the first message processor will be a `nextStep`, received from `snd`. This allows modes to form their own context of the dialog, like a person who understands your language. This will be the first thing you will ask next time.

We can chain simple modes into complex ones with the help of such combinators. Scala allows us to use fancy syntax for chains: any method with one parameter can be used as a binary operator. So, if we define the `or` method in `ChatbotMode`, we will be able to combine our modes:

```
def or(other: ChatbotMode): ChatbotMode = Or(this,other)
```

And later in `main`, we can write this:

```
def createInitMode() = (Bye or CurrentDate or CurrentTime) otherwise
InterestingIgnore
```

`Otherwise` looks very similar, with one difference: the second mode must always be second.

When we write one, it looks like this.

```
def main(args: Array[String]): Unit = {

 val name = StdIn.readLine("Hi! What is your name? ")
 println(s" $name, tell me something interesting, say 'bye' to end the
talk")

 var mode = createInitMode()
 var c = Processed("",mode,false)
 while(!c.endOfDialog){
   c = c.nextMode.process(effects.input.read(),effects) match {
    case next@Processed(_,_,_) => next
    case Failed => // impossible, but let be here as extra control.
       Processed("Sorry, can't understand you",c.nextMode,false)
   }
   effects.output.writeln(c.answer)
 }
}
```

We can make this a little better: let's move first the interaction (where the program asks the user for their name) to mode.

Now, we'll move the frst interaction to mode.

Here, we will make mode, which remembers your name and can make one for you.

1. Define a new object, which implements the chatbot trait and when running the first words, my name is, accepts a name and answers hi, and then tells you your name:

```
case class Name(name:String) extends ChatbotMode {

  override def process(message: String, effects: EffectsProvider):
LineStepResult = {
      message match {
        case "my name" =>
          if (name.isEmpty) {
            effects.output.write("What is your name?")
            val name = effects.input.read()
            Processed("hi, $name", Name(name), false)
          } else {
            Processed(s"your name is $name",this,false)
          }
        case _ => Failed
      }
    }
}
```

2. Add this object to the sequence of nodes in main:

```
def createInitMode() = (Bye or CurrentDate or CurrentTime or
Name("")) otherwise InterestingIgnore
```

3. Add a test with this functionality to testcase. Notice the usage of custom effects:

 For full code, refer to Code Snippets/Lesson 2.scala file.

```
test("step of my-name") {
  val mode = Chatbot3.createInitMode()
  val effects = new EffectsProvider {
    override val output: UserOutput = (message: String) => {}

    override def input: UserInput = () => "Joe"

    override def currentDate(): LocalDate = Chatbot3.effects.
currentDate()

    override def currentTime(): LocalTime = Chatbot3.effects.
currentTime()
  }
```

```
val result1 = mode.process("my name",effects)
assert(result1.isInstanceOf[Processed])
val r1 = result1.asInstanceOf[Processed]
assert(r1.answer == "Hi, Joe")
val result2 = r1.nextMode.process("my name",effects)
assert(result2.isInstanceOf[Processed])
val r2 = result2.asInstanceOf[Processed]
assert(r2.answer == "Your name is Joe")

}
```

Function Calls

Now, we'll look at how function calls are implemented in Scala.

Syntax Goodies

Scala provides flexible syntax and it is worth dedicating a few minutes to this concept.

Named Parameters

The following is a function, f(a:Int, b:Int). We can call this function using the named parameter syntax: f(a = 5, b=10). If we swap the parameters but leave the correct names, the method will still be correct.

It is possible to combine positional and named function calls—the first few arguments can be positional.

For example:

```
def f(x:Int, y:Int) = x*2 + y

f(x=1,y=2) // 4
f(y=1,x=2) // 5
```

Default Parameters

When specifying a function, we can set default parameters. Then, later, when we call this function, we can omit parameters and the compiler will substitute defaults:

```
def f(x:Int, y:Int=2) = x*2 + y

f(1) // 4
```

It is possible to create a comfortable API with the help of the combination of named and default arguments. For example, for case classes with N components, the compiler generates a copy method with N arguments; all of them have defaults:

```
case class Person(firstName: String, lastName: String)
val p1 = Person("Jon","Bull")
val p2 = p1.copy(firstName = "Iyan")
```

Now, let's transform code in the `Or` and `Otherwise` combinators to use the `copy` method instead of the `Processed` constructor.

1. Change the case expression to type, checking `(processed:Processed)` or adding the `bind` variable to the case class pattern `(processed@ Processed(... ))`

2. In the case body, use the `copy` method instead of the `Processed` constructor:

    ○   The resulting code should be as per the following cases:

    ○   If the student uses type check in the case expression:

    ```
    case processed:Processed =>
       processed.copy(nextMode = Or(processed.nextMode,snd))
    ```

    ○   If the student uses bind variable:

    ```
    case processed@Processed(answer,nextMode,endOfDialog) =>
       processed.copy(nextMode = Or(nextMode,snd))
    ```

3. Do the same transformation for the second match statement.

The full code looks like this:

```
case class Or(frs: ChatbotMode, snd: ChatbotMode) extends ChatbotMode
{
 override def process(message: String,
         effects: EffectsProvider): LineStepResult = {
 frs.process(message, effects) match {
   case processed@Processed(answer,nextMode,endOfDialog) =>
     processed.copy(nextMode = Or(nextMode,snd))
   case Failed => snd.process(message,effects) match {
     case processed@Processed(answer,nextMode,endOfDialog) =>
       processed.copy(nextMode=Or(nextMode,frs))
     case Failed => Failed
   }
 }
 }
}
```

Currying Forms (Multiple Argument Lists)

Currying is a term used for describing the transformation of a function with multiple arguments into a function with one argument. We will describe this process in detail in the next chapter.

It is vital for syntax that we can use multiple argument lists:

```
def f1(x:Int,y:Int) = x + y
def f2(x:Int)(y:Int) = x + y
```

Here, f2 is in its curried form. It has the same semantics as f1, but can be called with a different syntax. This is useful when you need visually separate arguments.

Special Magic Methods

The following table shows the various magic methods:

x.apply(y,z)	x(y,z)	
x.update(y,z)	x(y)=z	
x.y_=(z)	x.y=z	Method y must be also defined.
x.unary-	-x	The same for +, ~, !
x = x + y	x += y	The same for -,*,/,|,&

Implementing + in CartesianPoint

Open the previous project from *Lesson2* and implement + in CartesianPoint.

1. In your IDE, open the previous project (4-project, named coordinates).
2. In the CartesianPoint.scala file, add the + method with the following definition:

```
def +(v:CartesianPoint) = CartesianPoint(x+v.x,y+v.y)
```

Parameter-Passing Mode

In this section, we will learn the types of parameters which are in passing mode: by value, by name, and by need.

By Value

In previous chapters, we used default the parameters of passing mode: `by value`, which is the default in most programming languages.

In this model, the function call expression is evaluated in the following manner:

- First, all arguments are evaluated from left to right

- Then, the function is called, and parameters are referred to as evaluated arguments:

```
def f(x:Int) = x + x + 1

f({ println("A "); 10 }) // A res: 21
```

- Sometimes, we hear about Java parameter mode, where values are passed `by value`, and references are `by reference` (for example, if we pass `reference` to an object as a `value`)

By Name

The essence of the `by name` parameter passing mode is that arguments are not evaluated before the function call, but every time the name of the parameter is used in the target function:

```
def f(x: =>Int) = x + x + 1

f({ println("A "); 10 }) // A A res: 21
```

The name term comes to us from Algol68: passing parameters by name was described as a substitution of name by the parameter body. This was a challenge for compiler writers for many years.

By name parameters can be used for defining control-flow expressions:

```
def until(condition: =>Boolean)(body: =>Unit) =
{
 while(!condition) body
}
```

Note that constructor parameters can also be passed by name:

```
class RunLater(x: =>Unit)
{
 def run(): Unit = x
}
```

By Need

`By need` evaluates the parameter once, only if it is necessary. This can be emulated with the by name call and lazy val:

```
def f(x: =>Int): Int = {
 lazy val nx = x
 nx + nx + 1
}
f({ println("A "); 10 }) // A res: 21
```

We see the lazy modifier for val. A lazy value is evaluated at the time of the first usage and then stored in memory as a value.

Lazy values can be components of traits, classes, and objects: this is this usual way to define lazy initialization.

Creating a Runnable Construction

Let's create a runnable construction, with the same syntax as `Scalatest FunSuite`, and `executor`, which will return `true`, if the code inside the `test` argument was evaluated without exceptions.

1. Define the parent class with variables where the code will be captured. One possible example is as follows:

```
class DSLExample {

  val name: String = "undefined"
  var code: ()=>Unit = { () => () }


}
```

2. Define the function with the name and by-name parameter, which will fill this variable:

```
def test(testName:String)(testCode: =>Unit):Unit = {
 name = testName
 code = () => testCode
}
```

3. Define `executor` method, which uses named parameter inside try/catch block.

```
def run(): Boolean = {
 try {
  code()
  true
 } catch {
  case ex: Exception =>
   ex.printStackTrace()
   false
  }
}
```

Printing the log Argument to the Console and File

Let's create a `log` statement, which prints arguments to the console and to file, but only if the parameter with the name enabled in the logger constructor is set to true.

1. Define the `logger` with the parameter and class. The signature must be something like this:

```
class Logger(outputStream:PrintStream, dupToConsole: Boolean,
enabled: Boolean) {

    …. Inset method here


}
```

2. Define the method with the by-need parameter, which is only used when the logger is enabled:

```
def log(message: => String): Unit = {
  if (enabled) {
    val evaluatedMessage = message
    if (dupToConsole) {
      Console.println(evaluatedMessage)
    }
    outputStream.println(evaluatedMessage)
  }
}
```

Let's make `mode` command, which understands the `store name` definition and `remind` definition.

3. Define a new object which implements the `ChatbotMode` trait and has a data structure (a sealed trait which forms a linked list) as a state.

4. On the processing `store`, modify the state and answer `ok`. On processing, `remind` – answer.

5. Add test to `testcase`.

Summary

We have now reached the end of this chapter. In this chapter, we covered the object-oriented aspects of Scala such as classes, objects, pattern matching, self-types, case classes, and so on. We also implemented object-oriented concepts that we learned in our chatbot application.

In the next chapter, we will cover functional programming with Scala and how object-oriented and functional approaches complete each other. We will also cover generic classes, which are often used with pattern matching. We will also cover how to create user-defined pattern matching and why is it useful.

3
Functions

In the previous chapter, we covered the object-oriented aspects of Scala, such as classes, objects, pattern matching, self-types, case classes, and so on. We also implemented object-oriented concepts that we learned in our chatbot application.

In this chapter, we will cover functional programming with Scala and how object-oriented and functional approaches complete each other. We will also cover generic classes, which are often used with pattern matching. We will also cover how to create user-defined pattern matching and why is it useful.

By the end of this chapter, you will be able to:

- Identify the basics of functional programming
- Identify the basics of generic types in Scala
- Implement user-defined pattern matching
- Recognize and use functional compositional patterns

Functions

In this section, we will introduce the fundamentals of functional programming, such as function values and high-order functions.

Function Values

What is a function? We are familiar with methods, which must be defined in a scope (class or objects):

```
def f1(x:Int, y:Int): Int =  x + y
```

In Scala, we can also define a function value:

```
val f2: (Int,Int) => Int = (x,y) => (x+y).
```

Here, we define the function value, with a type of `(Int,Int) => Int`. Of course, as with all type declarations, the type can be omitted if it can be deduced from the context. So, an alternative syntax for this can be:

```
val f2 = (x:Int,y:Int) => (x+y).
```

Both `f1(1,2)` and `f2(1,2)` will force evaluation. The difference between `f1` and `f2` is that the second is a value, which can be stored in a variable or passed to another function.

Functions which accept other functions as parameters are named high-order functions, for example:

```
def twice(f: Int => Int): Int => Int = x => f(f(x))
```

This function returns functions, which apply parameters twice. An example of this usage is as follows:

```
val incr2 = (x:Int) => x+2
val incr4 = twice(incr2)
incr4(2)    //==6
twice(x=>x+2)(3)    // 7
```

In general, the syntax for function definitions is as follows:

```
val fname: (X1 … XN)  => Y = (x1:X1, … x2:XN) => expression
```

The type signature can be omitted if it is possible to deduce types from the context.

Now, let's look at how to define a function variable.

Define the function variable in the REPL of IDE worksheet:

```
val f:  Int=>Int = x => x+1
```

Function from an OO Point of View

When looking at Scala sources, we will see the following definition:

```
trait Function1[-T1, +R] {

  def apply(v1: T1): R
  ....
}
```

Here, `Function1` is a base trait for a function with one argument. `Function1` has one abstract method: `apply`. Scala provides syntax sugar for the call of the `apply` method with syntax.

`T1` and `R` are type parameters of `Function1`. `T1` is a type of the first argument, while `R` is a result type.

Symbols before type parameters [`-T1, +R`] mean `contravariance` and `covariance` of parameters; we will speak about one in detail later. For now, let's write a definition:

```
F[T]   covariant,   iff   A <: B =>  F[A]  <:  F[B]
  F[T]    contravariant  iff  A >: B => F[A] <: F[B]
```

The value of a function with one argument, `f: A => B`, is just an instance of a trait, `Function1[A,B]`. For functions with two arguments, we have `Function2[T1,T2,R]` and so on. We can rewrite an example with `twice` using OO facilities in the next form:

```
//   val twice(f:Int=>Int):Int=>Int = x => f(f(x))
object  Twice extends Function1[Function1[Int,Int],Function1[Int,Int]]
{

  def apply(f: Function1[Int,Int]): Function1[Int,Int] =
    new Function1[Int,Int] {
      def apply(x:Int):Int =   f.apply(f.apply(x))
    }

}
```

Here, we define the `Twice` object with the same behavior of the previously described function:

```
val incr2 = (x:Int) => x+2
val incr4 = Twice(incr2)
incr4(2)   //=6
Twice(x=>x+2)(5)  //=9
```

To summarize, we can say:

- The function value is an instance of an appropriative function trait.
- The call of a function value is a call of the `apply()` method in a function trait.

Now, it's time to create a few functions.

1. Open a blank worksheet in your project.

2. Define the function which accepts the binary function and arguments, and return an application of such a function:

    ```
    g(f: (Int,Int)=>Int, x: Int, y:Int): Int = f(x,y)
    ```

3. Make the syntax better by reformulating the function using currying:

    ```
    g(f: (Int,Int)=>Int)( x: Int, y:Int): Int = f(x,y)
    ```

4. Partial application: Write the `fix` function, which accepts binary function and an argument and returns an unary function, which will apply the placed function and argument. For example, with definition g as : `val g = fix1((x,y)=>x+y,3)`.

5. `g(2)` should be evaluated to `5`.

    ```
    fix(f: (Int,Int)=>Int)( x: Int): Int => Int = y => f(x,y)
    ```

Conversions

We have methods and functional values, which can do the same thing. It is logical to expect a conversion between them, for example, the ability to assign a method to a functional variable or pass a function as an OO interface.

Scala provides a special syntax for converting a method to a value. We just need to add the underscore (_) after the name of the method.

For example:

```
val printFun = Console.print _
```

Also, a functional value can be implicitly converted to a so-called SAM (Single Abstract Method) trait. A SAM trait has only one abstract method, and we can pass a function in its context, where the SAM trait is required (and the function type conforms to the method signature).:

```
val th = new Thread(()=> println(s"threadId=${Thread.currentThread().
getId}"))
th.start()
```

Here, we pass the function with zero parameters to the `Thread` constructor, which accepts the `Runnable` interface.

In Scala, we have three different ways of implementing deferred call functionality.

Defining and Measuring the Time of a Unit Function

Define a function which accepts a function which runs a unit function and measures the time in nanoseconds. How long does this take? Implement this in three different ways.

1. Write a function which accepts other functions. Run one and measure the execution time:

```
def measure1(f: Unit => Unit): Long = {
  val startTime = System.nanoTime()
  f()
  val endTime = System.nanoTime()
  endTime - startTime
}
```

2. Write a function which accepts the by-name parameter. Run one and measure the execution time:

```
def measure2(f: => Unit): Long = {
  val startTime = System.nanoTime()
  f
  val endTime = System.nanoTime()
  endTime - startTime
}
```

3. Write an object which extends the `Function1` trait and do the same in the `apply` method:

```
object Measure3 extends Function1[Unit=>Unit,Long]
{
  override def apply(f: Unit=>Unit) = {
        val startTime = System.nanoTime()
```

```
        f()
        val endTime = System.nanoTime()
        endTime - startTime
    }
  }
```

Syntax Sugar in a Function Definition

Sometimes, writing expressions such as `x => x+1` look too verbose. To solve this, syntax sugar exists, which allows you to write small functional expressions in a compact and idiomatic way. Don't write the left part at all, and, while writing, use _ (underscore) instead of an argument. The first underscore means the first argument, the second underscore means the second argument, and so on:

```
  _ + 1   is a shortcut for  x =>  x+1,   _ + _  -- for (x,y) => x + y.
```

Some functions such as `(x,y) => x*x + y` can't be represented in such a notation.

Partial Functions

Partial functions are better known as partially defined functions — some values exist in the domain of the function input, where this function is undefined.

Let's look at a simplified definition:

```
trait PartialFunction[-A, +B] extends (A => B) {

  /** Checks if a value is contained in the function's domain.
    *
    * @param x    the value to test
    * @return `'''true'''`, iff `x` is in the domain of this function,
`'''false'''` otherwise.
    */
  def isDefinedAt(x: A): Boolean
}
```

Along with the apply method we have a `isDefinedAt` method, which returns `true` if our function is applicable for an argument, and a special syntax:

```
val pf: PartialFunction[Int,String] = {
  case 0 => "zero"
  case 1 => "one"
  case 2 => "two"
  case x:Int if x>0 => "many"
}
```

```
pf.isDefinedAt(1)   - true
pf.isDefinedAt(-1)  - false

pf(-1)  throws exceptions.
```

We can combine a few partial functions into a new set of standard combinators — orElse:

```
val pf1: PartialFunction[Int,String] = pf orElse { case _ => "other" }
```

Note that type annotation is needed to give a correct context for type deduction. Otherwise, the compiler will not be able to deduce the type of inline function argument.

One useful combinator — andThen, which allows building pipelines, is also necessary:

```
pf andThen (_.length)(1)
```

Now, define a function which accepts a function and provides a transformed function. For example, let the input function be f: Int => Int, and let's build g(f): g(f)(x) = f(x) + x. If f is not defined at x, g(f) must not be defined either.

1. Copy the following class:

    ```
    class g1(f:PartialFunction[Int,Int]) extends
    PartialFunction[Int,Int] {

        override def isDefinedAt(x: Int) =
                f.isDefinedAt(x)

        override def apply(x: Int) =
                f(x) + x
    }
    ```

2. Or as a case-expression with an if clause:

    ```
                    def g2(f:PartialFunction[Int,Int]):PartialFunction[
    Int,Int] = {
                        case x if f.isDefinedAt(x) => f(x)+x
                    }
    ```

We'll now implement a partial function for constructing an association between names and values.

1. Write a function for a pair as a class with parameters (name,value), which is defined only if the argument is equal to name:

    ```
    class NVPair(name: String, value: String) extends
    PartialFunction[String,String] {

        override def isDefinedAt(x: String): Boolean = (x==name)
    ```

```
        override def apply(x: String): String = {
          if (x==name) value else throw new MatchError()
        }
      }
```

2. Use the `orElse` combinator to combine such pairs into a bigger function:

```
val f = new NVPair("aa","bb") orElse new NVPair("cc","dd")
```

Exploring Pattern Matching

Now we will return to pattern matching and learn about extending capabilities behind case classes. As you will remember from the previous chapter, we can use pattern matching against case classes, where fields of a class can be bound to the variables in the scope of an appropriative case clause. Can we do this for our non-case classes and embed our own custom logic for matching?

In this section, we will learn how to write our own pattern matcher and get acquainted with some standard generic classes which are often used with pattern matching.

Now, let's get started with the minimal example.

1. First, we write the following code in the IDE:

```
case class Wrapper(x:Int)

w match {
  case Wrapper(x) => doSomething(x)
}
```

2. Under the hood, the compiler compiled this to the next intermediate form:

```
val container = Wrapper.unapply(w)
if (container.isDefined) {
  val x = container.get
  doSomething(x)
}
```

  °   The `unapply` method of the companion object is called, which must return the class with the methods `get` and `isDefined`.

3. When we have more than one binding variable, the resulting container should contain a tuple. For example, for the point intermediate form, this will be the resulting code:

```
val container = Point.unapply(p)
if (container.isDefined) {
  val (x,y) = container.get
  doSomething(x,y)
}
```

  ◦   The standard Scala library provides the `Option` type, although it is possible to define your own type with such methods (which can be useful in some heavy optimization scenarios).

4. Define the class:

```
sealed abstract class Option[+A]  {

  def isEmpty: Boolean
  def isDefined: Boolean = !isEmpty
  def get: A

  // … other methods

}

final case class Some[+A](value: A) extends Option[A] {
  def isEmpty = false
  def get = value
}

case object None extends Option[Nothing] {
  def isEmpty = true
  def get = throw new NoSuchElementException("None.get")
}
```

  ◦   Here, we see the algebraic type (such as the hierarchy of case classes/objects) with the generic type parameter: A. You may have heard of the abbreviation GADT (Generic Algebraic Data Type) when referring to such constructs.

  ◦   Informal value of `Option[A]` – the container from one or zero elements, or elements which can or cannot exist. Some(a) – when an element exists, None – for its absence.

  ◦   `None` extends `Option[Nothing]`. Nothing is a `minimal` type in the Scala typesystem, which is a subtype of any type.

5. So, to define the custom pattern matcher, we need to create an object with the `unapply` method and put logic inside of it which returns a binding variable (or a tuple with binding variables) in an option container:

```
case class Point(x:Int, y:Int)
```

6. Let's define the pattern matcher `Diagonal`, which will match only points situated in the diagonal:

```
object Diagonal {
  def unapply(p:Point): Option[Int] =
    if (p.x == p.y) Some(p.x) else None
}
```

We'll now implement the `unapply` custom.

1. Define object `Axis` (Numbered Bullet)

2. Define method `unapply` (Numbered Bullet END)

3. Determinate, if object is on X axis(Apply BULLET INSIDE BULLET to all three points)

4. Determinate, if object is on Y axis

5. Otherwise, return `None`.

Binding a Sequence of Variables in the Pattern Matcher

Sometimes, we need a particular type of pattern matcher where the number of binding variables can vary. For example, regular expressions in standard Scala library are as follows:

```
val r1 = "([\\d]+)".r
val r2 = "([\\d]+)  ([^\\W]*)".r

v match {
  case r1(x) => "1"
  case r2(x,y) => "2"
}
```

Here, we can see that that r1 is matched with one variable, but r2 uses two binding variables. Another convention exists for this case: a companion object should provide the `unapplySeq` method instead of `unapply`, which returns a sequence wrapped in an option.

We will learn more about sequences during the next chapter, but for now we can say that Seq[A] – is a generic trait for sequences. The apply operator in sequences works as index access (for example, seq(n) returns the nth element of the sequence, and it is possible to create default sequence using the Seq companion class, Seq(1,2,3).

Let's now implement the custom unapplySeq method. This is defined on strings and returns a sequence of words.

1. Define the Words object.

2. Define the unapplySeq method. Transform the array to seq, using the .toSeq method in Scala Array:

```scala
object Words {

  def unapplySeq(arg: String):Option[Seq[String]] = {
  val array = arg.split("\\W+")
  if (array.size == 1 && array(0).isEmpty ) {
    None
  } else {
    Some(array.toSeq)
  }
  }
}
```

3. Write a test which compares words for the following strings:

```scala
    "1",    "AA AA",   "AA    AA",   "ABC CBA",   "A B C D E      F G
X-L",""
"AAA     AAA" match {
  case Words(x,y) => (x,y)
}
```

   ○ Sometimes, when binding variables into sequence, we don't need var for each value in the sequence, but only the first value and the rest of the sequence.

4. We can use the pattern with the syntax for a variable function call in a pattern, for example:

```scala
object AsSeq
{

  def unapplySeq(x:Array[Int]):Option[Seq[Int]] = {
    Some(x)
  }
}
```

```
}

Array(1,2,3,6) match {
  case AsSeq(h, _*) => h
}
```

Partial Functions in Practice

Now that we have learned a lot about functions and pattern matching, let's apply our theoretical knowledge to practical programming.

Let's get our chatbot, which we developed during the previous chapter, and change the modes to partial functions instead of classes.

 Open /Lesson 3/5-project in the supplement materials and import the project into the IDE.

Representing ChatbotMode as a Partial Function

Let's navigate to the scala file package in com.packt.courseware.14:

```
package com.packt.courseware.14

package object modes {
  type ChatbotMode = PartialFunction[(String,EffectsProvider),Process
ed]

    ...
}
```

Here, we see the package object, which was not mentioned previously in our chapters.

The package object is an object which is associated with a package. When you import a package with a wildcard, then you import the current scope content of the package object if one exists.

So, the package object is a good way to store some utility definitions and functions, which should be available in a package.

The next sentence is a type alias for `ChatbotMode`: we define one as a partial function from (`String`, `EffectsProvider`) to `Processed`.

As you will remember, `Processed` is a `LineStepResult` which is a trait, united with Processed or Failed. With partial functions, we don't need a `Failed` variant; instead, `isDefined` in our mode will be set to `false`.

Now let's look at some simple mode:

```
val bye: ChatbotMode = { case ("bye", eff) => Processed("bye", bye,
true) }
```

So, we can write partial functions just as we do `vars`.

In the previous version, we have `OrMode`, which combines modes in combination. Can we do the same with partial functions?

```
def or(frs:ChatbotMode, snd: ChatbotMode): ChatbotMode = {
  val frsPost = frs.andThen(p => p.copy(nextMode = or(p.
nextMode,snd)))
  val sndPost = snd.andThen(p => p.copy(nextMode = or(p.
nextMode,frs)))
  frsPost orElse sndPost
}
```

We use the `andThen` combinator for postprocessing the result of applying `frs` and `snd` in order to insert `nextMode` in the or chain and return those functions in the `orElse` combinator.

So, as we can see, modes can be described with the help of partial functions. The resultant code is a little shorter, but we only lose the fancy syntax for combining modes.

The main mode now looks like this:

```
import modes._
def createInitMode() = otherwise (
  or(StoreRemindCommand.empty, or(bye,or(currentDate,currentTime))),
  interestingIgnore)
```

Let's now implement partial functions. In l4, some modes are removed from the source code. Can you move them back, in the form of partial functions?

Steps for Completion:

1. Open Lesson 3/5-project.

2. Implement the currentTime, otherwise, and interestingIgnore modes.

3. Ensure that the tests are running.

Implementing RemindStore as a Set of Partial Functions

Let's look at the implementation of RemindStore. Navigate to com/packt/courseware/l4/RemindCommand.scala.

Look at using regular expressions in patterns:

```
val StorePattern = raw"store ([^\W]+) (.*)".r;
val RemindPattern = raw"remind ([^\W]+)".r;

def process(state:RemindedState): ChatbotMode =
{
  case (StorePattern(n,v),effects) => Processed("ok",process(state.
store(n,v)),false)
  case (RemindPattern(n),effects) if state.isDefinedAt(n) => Processed
(state(n),process(state),false)
}
```

Note that RemindedState has a memory leak: what will be the behavior of the function when we ask our chatbot to store the same word a few times?

> A memory leak is a situation where we allocate an object but keep it accessible after usage.

Let's now find and fix a memory leak in StoreRemindCommand.

1. Open Lesson 3/5-project.

2. Analyze the case where we stored the same work a few times.

3. Consider how it's possible to write a unit test for this (★★★)?

4. Fix the memory leak.

As we have seen, it is possible to build modes in chatbot as partial functions.

Using Lifting for Conversations between Total and Partial Functions

Such a design has drawbacks:

The first drawback is that our partial function always accepts one parameter: a tuple of input and effects. This can be a source of confusion.

Also note that a decision where we process input or reject (and it will be passed to the next chain by a combinator) should be written twice: first in `isDefinedAt`, then in apply. In simple cases, this is hidden from us by case syntax, where `isDefinedAt` is produced automatically.

It looks like a loss of a binary operator syntax is the third problem. However, this is not a real problem. We will learn how it is possible to define our own syntax on third-party classes in *Chapter 5, Scala Type System*.

Can we have one point of decision and work with a partially defined value?

Let's look at the next method from the standard library:

```
trait PartialFunction[-A, +B] extends (A => B) {
  ....

  /** Turns this partial function into a plain function returning an
  `Option` result.
   * @see      Function.unlift
   * @return   a function that takes an argument `x` to `Some(this(x))`
  if `this`
   *           is defined for `x`, and to `None` otherwise.
   */
  def lift: A => Option[B]

}
```

We can represent a partial function as a total function with the result wrapped in `Option`. For a combinator of partial functions, we have very similar methods to `Option`.

Let's change the design of our modes again.

Look at `Lesson 3/6-project`.

ChatbotMode is a trait once more:

```
trait ChatbotMode {

    def process(line:String,effects:EffectsProvider):Option[Processed]

    def or(other: ChatbotMode) = OrMode(this,other)

    def otherwise(other: ChatbotMode) = OtherwiseMode(this,other)

}
```

But we can define simple modes with the help of partial functions and transform one to our traits using the helper constructor:

```
object ChatbotMode
{
  def partialFunction(f:PartialFunction[String,Processed]):
ChatbotMode =
    { (line,effects) => f.lift(line) }
}
```

After that, we can do this:

```
val bye: ChatbotMode = ChatbotMode.partialFunction(
                    { case "bye" => Processed("bye", bye, true) })
```

Also note that we can initialize ChatbotMode from the function because ChatbotMode is a SAM type:

```
val interestingIgnore: ChatbotMode = ( line, effects ) =>
                    Some(Processed("interesting...",interestingIgn
ore,false))
```

Also, we can compare the implementation of OrMode with the previous variant, based on partial function combinators:

```
case class OrMode(frs:ChatbotMode, snd:ChatbotMode) extends
ChatbotMode {

  override def process(line: String, effects: EffectsProvider):
Option[Processed] = {
    frs.process(line,effects).map(
      p => p.copy(nextMode = OrMode(p.nextMode,snd))
    ) orElse snd.process(line,effects).map(
      p => p.copy(nextMode = OrMode(p.nextMode,frs))
    )
  }
}
```

As you can see, that structure is very similar: map used `andThen` instead in the partial function, and Option also uses `orElse`. We can say that the domains `PartialFunction[A,B]` and `Function[A,Option[B]]` are isomorphic.

There is a default transformer from a partial function to a function of an option, and it is named `lift`.

This is a method of a partial function:

```
{ case "bye" => Processed("bye", bye, true) }.lift
```

This will have the same effect as this:

```
x => if (x=="bye") Some(Processed("bye", bye, true)) else
None
```

Let's write an inverse transformer, `unlift`:

```
def unlift[X,Y](f: X => Option[Y]):PartialFunction[X,Y] = new
PartialFunction[X,Y] {

 override def isDefinedAt(x: X) =
 f(x).isDefined

  override def apply(x: X) =
      f(x) match {
            case Some(y) => y
         }
}
```

It is a good practice to provide more efficient chain operations, for example:

```
override def applyOrElse[A1 <: X, B1 >: Y](x: A1, default: A1 => B1):
B1 =
    f(x) match {
          case Some(y) => y
          case None => default(x)
      }
```

Here, we call the underlying `f` once.

Let's now add a simple TODO list to our chatbot.

We will change our model of evaluation by allowing more than one mode to evaluate input. A combinator will choose the best evaluation.

1. Open `Lesson 3/6-project`.
2. Add the `Processed, relevance` parameter between 0 and 1.
3. Modify the `or` combinator to evaluate both of the child modes and select answer, based on its relevance.
4. Add a test to the `test` cases.

Summary

In this chapter, we have covered functional programming with Scala and how object-oriented and functional approaches complete each other. We also covered generic classes, which are often used with pattern matching. Finally, we covered how to create user-defined pattern matching and learned why is it useful.

In the next chapter, we'll cover important Scala collections such as `Sets` and `Maps`. We'll also discuss mutable and immutable collections and their applicability in Scala code.

4

Scala Collections

In the previous chapter, we covered functional programming with Scala and how object-oriented and functional approaches complete each other. We also covered generic classes, which are often used with pattern matching. Finally, we covered how to create user-defined pattern matching and why it is useful.

In this chapter, we will cover the Scala Collection library. We will start by learning how to work with lists, which will make us familiar with some design principles of the whole collections library. Afterward, we'll generalize to sequences and cover some more relevant data structures. At the end, we'll look at how collections relate to monads and how we can use that knowledge to make some powerful abstractions in our code.

Scala's collection library is very rich, being comprised of data structures for very different use cases and performance considerations. It is particularly rich in immutable data structures, which we will be covering in greater detail during this chapter.

Collections available in the Scala collection library inherit from common high-level abstract classes and traits and, as such, share some common functionalities, which makes working with them easier once you become familiar with certain methods and design principles.

By the end of this chapter, you will be able to:

- Identify the Scala collections available in the standard library
- Identify how to abstract sequences by using higher-order functions
- Implement the important design principles for working with Scala collections

Working with Lists

Lists are probably the most commonly used data structures in Scala programs. Learning how to work with lists is important both from a data structure standpoint but also as an entry point to designing programs around recursive data structures.

Constructing Lists

In order to be able to use lists, one must learn how to construct them. Lists are recursive in nature, and build upon two basic building blocks: Nil (representing the empty list) and :: (pronounced cons, from the cons function of most Lisp dialects).

We will now create Lists in Scala:

1. Start the Scala REPL, which should provide you with a prompt:

   ```
   $ scala
   ```

2. Create a list of strings using the following:

   ```
   scala> val listOfStrings = "str1" :: ("str2" :: ("str3" :: Nil))
   listOfStrings: List[String] = List(str1, str2, str3)
   ```

3. Show that the :: operation is the right associative by omitting the parentheses and getting the same result:

   ```
   scala> val listOfStrings = "str1" :: "str2" :: "str3" :: Nil
   listOfStrings: List[String] = List(str1, str2, str3)
   ```

4. Create lists of different types.

5. Show that the apply method of the List companion object offers a convenient way to create a list from a variable number of arguments:

   ```
   scala> val listOfStrings = List("str1", "str2", "str3")
   listOfStrings: List[String] = List(str1, str2, str3)
   ```

If you are wondering how is it possible for the :: operator to be right-associative, note that the associativity of an operator is determined by the operator's last character. Operators ending in a colon : are right-associative. All other operators are left-associative. Since :: ends with a colon, it is right-associative.

Operations on Lists

The List class provides the head, tail, and isEmpty methods. head returns the first element of the list, while the tail method returns the list without its first element. The isEmpty method returns true if the list is empty, and false otherwise. head and tail are only defined for non-empty lists and throw an exception on empty ones.

> Calling head and tail in empty lists (such as Nil.head and Nil.tail) throws an exception.
>
> To implement the evenInts method with the following signature, use the following code:
> ```
> def evenInts(l: List[Int]): List[Int]
> ```

The method should return a list with all even integers of list l. Use the head, tail, and isEmpty methods of List. A possible solution for this problem is the following:

```
def evenInts(l: List[Int]): List[Int] = {
  if (l.isEmpty) l
  else if (l.head % 2 == 0) l.head :: evenInts(l.tail)
  else evenInts(l.tail)
}
```

Pattern Matching on Lists

Pattern matching is a powerful mechanism for checking a value against a pattern in Scala and provides an idiomatic way to decompose lists. You can pattern match on ::, which mimics the list structure, or on List(...) to match all of the list's values.

Let's experiment with pattern matching in the Scala REPL. Make sure to show examples of both pattern matching with List(...) and with ::.

One possible example to show is:

```
val l = List(1, 2, 3, 4, 5)
List(a, b, c, d, e) = l
val h :: t = l
```

Using pattern matching is generally more idiomatic than using if and else to structure programs.

Now, we will implement the method `evenInts` again. This time, we will not use the `head`, `tail`, and `isEmpty` methods of `List`:

1. Open the file where we have written the `evenInts` method.

2. Do not use the `head`, `tail`, and `isEmpty` methods of `list`.

3. A possible solution for this problem is the following:

```
def evenInts(l: List[Int]): List[Int] = l match {
  case h :: t if h % 2 == 0 => h :: evenInts(t)
  case _ :: t => evenInts(t)
  case Nil => Nil
}
```

First-Order Methods on List

The `List` class provides various helpful first-order methods. A first-order method is one that does not take a function as an argument. We'll cover some of the most-used methods in the following subsection.

Appending and Concatenation

We've learned about `::` to append an element at the head of a list. If we want to append an element at the end of a list, we can use the `:+` operator. In order to concatenate two lists, we can use the `:::` operator. Note, however, that the `:+` operator has a time complexity of `O(n)`, where `n` is the number of elements in the list. The `:::` operator has a time complexity of `O(n)`, `n` being the number of elements in the first list. Note that the `:::` operator also has right-associativity, like the `::` operator.

Example code:

```
scala> val a = List(1, 2, 3)
a: List[Int] = List(1, 2, 3)

scala> val b = List(4, 5, 6)
b: List[Int] = List(4, 5, 6)
scala> val c = a ::: b
c: List[Int] = List(1, 2, 3, 4, 5, 6)

scala> val d = b :+ 7
d: List[Int] = List(4, 5, 6, 7)
```

Taking the Length of a List

Taking the length of a list is a useful operation. All lists have a definite size and, as such, they provide the `length` method that returns their size. We'll be covering potentially infinite data structures in another topic.

Note that `length` is an expensive operation on lists, as it needs to traverse the whole list to find its end, taking time proportional to the number of elements in the list.

Reversing a List

If you require frequent access to the end of a list, it is convenient to reverse it once and work with the result. The `reverse` method creates a new list with the elements of the original list reversed. The reverse method has linear complexity.

Prefixes and Suffixes

The `take` and `drop` methods of `List` return arbitrary prefixes or suffixes of a list. They both take an integer as an argument: the number of elements to take or drop, respectively.

Example code:

```
scala> val a = List(1, 2, 3, 4, 5)
a: List[Int] = List(1, 2, 3, 4, 5)

scala> val b = a.take(2)
b: List[Int] = List(1, 2)

scala> val c = a.drop(2)
c: List[Int] = List(3, 4, 5)
```

Element Selection

Even though it is not a common operation for lists, the `List` class supports random element selection through its apply method:

```
scala> val a = List(1, 2, 3, 4, 5)
a: List[Int] = List(1, 2, 3, 4, 5)

scala> a.apply(2)
res0: Int = 3
```

Since apply is implicitly inserted when an object appears in the function position in a method call, we can also do:

```
scala> a(2)
res1: Int = 3
```

Display

Use toString to get the canonical string representation of a list:

```
scala> val a = List(1, 2, 3, 4, 5)
a: List[Int] = List(1, 2, 3, 4, 5)

scala> a.toString
res0: String = List(1, 2, 3, 4, 5)
```

The mkString method is a bit more flexible as it allows you to specify the prefix to print before all elements, the separator to print between elements, and the suffix to print after all elements. The mkString method has two overloaded variants which allow you to drop the prefix and suffix arguments if they're empty strings. You can also call mkString without arguments if you want an empty string as a separator:

```
scala> a.mkString("[", ", ", "]")
res1: String = [1, 2, 3, 4, 5]
scala> a.mkString(", ")
res2: String = 1, 2, 3, 4, 5

scala> a.mkString
res3: String = 12345
```

Refer to the Scaladoc for the scala.collection.immutable. List class at https://www.scala-lang.org/api/ current/scala/collection/immutable/List.html. If you are interested in other useful methods, you can take a look at what the class has to offer.

Activity: Creating a New Mode for Chatbot Using Lists

In this activity, we will be building a new mode for the Chatbot that we created on the first day of this book. This new mode will be capable of keeping and updating a `todo` list of entries. We will be using `lists` as the primary data structure to hold our information, and we want to support at least the following commands:

- `todo list`: Lists all current items the bot is currently aware of.

- `todo new <item description>`: Inserts a new TODO item with the provided description.

- `todo done <item number>`: Removes the item numbered <item number> from the list. The number of the item should be shown when using `todo` list.

- `todo done <item description>`: Removes the item whose description matches <item description>.

1. Start by defining a new class that extends `ChatbotMode`. It's enough to model our TODO list items as strings, so our new mode could just be defined as `case class TodoList(todos: List[String]) extends ChatbotMode`.

2. Implement the required `process` method. Regexes might come in handy to parse the `line` argument. Depending on the provided input, we want to create a new instance of `TodoList` with the value of `todos` possibly modified. Return `None` in invalid inputs (unrecognizable commands or attempts to delete a non-existent item, for example).

3. Experiment with your newly defined mode in the previously implemented Chatbot. See how well it plays with the other already defined modes.

In this section, we covered lists in the perspective of one of the major workhorses of Scala programs. We've learned the operations we can perform on lists and covered some idiomatic ways to handle lists in Scala code.

Abstracting on Sequences

All Scala collections descend from a common trait called `Traversable`. The design adopted for Scala collections allows one to use higher-order functions similarly in nearly all collections, with proper return types in specific instances. Treating collections as sequences, or as containers of elements, allows one to use different data structures seamlessly.

The Traversable Trait

At the root of the collections hierarchy is the `Traversable` trait. The `Traversable` trait has a single abstract method:

```
def foreach[U](f: Elem => U)
```

The implementation of this method is sufficient for the `Traversable` trait to provide a series of useful higher-order methods.

We would like to focus on the `map` operations. The `map` method takes a function and applies it to every element of the collection.

Let's experiment with the `map` method in the Scala `REPL` and show how it applies to different types of collections. For now, create a function that multiplies an integer by 2 and apply it to a `List` and an `Array`:

```
scala> def f(i: Int) = i * 2
f: (i: Int)Int

scala> val l = List(1, 2, 3, 4).map(f)
l: List[Int] = List(2, 4, 6, 8)

scala> val a = Array(1, 2, 3, 4).map(f)
a: Array[Int] = Array(2, 4, 6, 8)
```

 Note that the return type of the map method varies according to the collection type it is called on.

The `flatMap` is slightly different. It takes a function from the type of elements in the collection to another collection which is then "flattened" in the returned collection.

As an example for the `flatMap` method, consider a function that takes an integer and creates a list of the integer size filled with 1. See what the return value is when that function is applied to a `list` via `map` and `flatMap`:

```
scala> def f(v: Int): List[Int] = if (v == 0) Nil else 1 :: f(v - 1)
f: (v: Int)List[Int]

scala> val l = List(1, 2, 3, 4).map(f)
l: List[List[Int]] = List(List(1), List(1, 1), List(1, 1, 1), List(1,
1, 1, 1))

scala> val ll = List(1, 2, 3, 4).flatMap(f)
ll: List[Int] = List(1, 1, 1, 1, 1, 1, 1, 1, 1, 1)
```

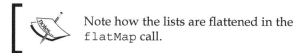

Note how the lists are flattened in the `flatMap` call.

These kind of operations closely resemble those of a `monad`.

A `monad` is a wrapper and a mechanism of sequencing operations. It provides two basic operations: `identity`, to wrap a value in a `monad`, and `bind`, to transform the underlying value of a `monad`. Monads will be covered in greater detail in *Chapter 7, Functional Idioms*, so don't worry if you don't quite grasp all the intricacies of them just yet.

The monadic mechanism of chaining `flatMaps` is so common that Scala provides a special syntax for it in for-comprehensions.

Monadic operations provide the programmer with a way to abstract and chain computations, where `map` and `flatMap` are the glue. The fact that `map` and `flatMap` are higher-order functions, in other words, they take other functions as arguments, allows the programmer to reuse components (`functions`) in their code.

Other important higher-order functions provided by the collections API are `folds`. Generically, folds provide ways to combine elements of a container with some binary operator. Folds are different from reduces in the sense that with fold you provide a starter value, whereas with `reduce` you only use the elements of the container. The `*Left` and `*Right` variants determine the order in which the elements are combined.

We will now implement sum on a List by using foldLeft. A possible solution to this problem is as follows:

```
def add(a: Int, b: Int) = a + b
def sum(l: List[Int]) = l.foldLeft(0)(add)
val res = sum(List(1, 2, 3, 4))
// Returns 10
```

Iterators

Right beneath the `Traversable` trait in the Scala collections hierarchy is the `Iterable` trait. An `Iterable` is a trait with a single abstract method:

```
def iterator: Iterator[A]
```

An `Iterator` provides a method to step through the collection's elements one by one. One important thing to note is that an `Iterator` is mutable, as most of its operations change its state. Namely, calling `next` on an `iterator` changes the in-place position of its `head`. Since an `Iterator` is simply something with `next` and `hasNext` methods, it is possible to create an iterator that isn't backed by any collection. Since all Scala collections also descend from `Iterable`, all of them have an `iterator` method to return an `Iterator` for its elements.

Streams

Streams provide an implementation of lazy lists where elements are only evaluated when they are needed. Streams also have a recursive structure, similar to `Lists`, based on the `#::` and `Stream.empty` building blocks (analogous to `::` and `Nil`). The biggest difference is that `#::` is lazy, and will only evaluate the tail when elements from it are needed. One important feature of Streams is that they're memoized, so values won't be recomputed if they were already computed once. The disadvantage of this is that if you keep hold of a reference to the head of a `Stream`, you will keep references to all the elements of the `Stream` computed so far.

Activity: Implementing Fibonacci Series Using Streams and Iterators

In mathematics, the sequence known as Fibonacci is defined by the number which generated by adding the two integers prior to the number. By definition, the first two integers in the series should be 1 and 1, or 0 and 1.

Implement the infinite sequence of Fibonacci numbers using Streams and Iterators:

```
lazy val fibIterator: Iterator[BigInt]
lazy val fibStream: Stream[BigInt]
```

One possible solution for these implementations is the following:

```
lazy val fibStream: Stream[BigInt] = BigInt(0) #:: BigInt(1) #::
fibStream.zip(fibStream.tail).map { n => n._1 + n._2 }
lazy val fibIterator = new Iterator[BigInt] {
  var v1 = 0
  var v2 = 1
  val hasNext = true
  def next = {
    val res = v1
    v1 = v2
```

```
    v2 = res + v1
    res
  }
}
```

In this section, we've covered `Traversables` as an abstract way to use and reason about collections in Scala. We also covered Iterators and Streams and their usefulness in implementing potentially infinite sequences.

Other Collections

Now that we've covered the List and some relevant `Traversables` in the Scala standard library, we should also visit some other useful collections Scala provides. Even though this section has less theoretical material, this means that we'll have more time on the final activities of the chapter.

Sets

`Sets` are `Iterables` that contain no duplicate elements. The `Set` class provides methods to check for the inclusion of an element in the collection, as well as combining different collections. Note that since `Set` inherits from `Traversable`, you can apply all the higher-order functions we've seen previously on it. Due to the nature of its `apply` method, a `Set` can be seen as a function of type `A => Boolean`, which returns `true` if the element is present in the set, and `false` otherwise.

Tuples

A tuple is a class capable of containing an arbitrary number of elements of different types. A tuple is created by enclosing its elements in parentheses. A tuple is typed according to the type of its elements.

Let's now create tuples in REPL and access their elements by following these steps:

1. Create some tuples in the REPL and access their elements.
2. Observe the type of the tuples created, and how it depends on the enclosing elements' types.
3. Use pattern matching as a way to destructure tuples.

The full code looks as follows:

```scala
scala> val tup = (1, "str", 2.0)
tup: (Int, String, Double) = (1,str,2.0)

scala> val (a, b, c) = tup
a: Int = 1
b: String = str
c: Double = 2.0

scala> tup._1
res0: Int = 1

scala> tup._2
res1: String = str

scala> tup._3
res2: Double = 2.0

scala> val pair = 1 -> "str"
pair: (Int, String) = (1,str)
```

Maps

A `Map` is an `Iterable` of tuples of size two (pairs of key/values), which are also called mappings or associations. A `Map` can't have repeated keys. One interesting fact about maps in Scala is that `Map[A, B]` extends `PartialFunction[A, B]`, so you can use a `Map` in places where you need a `PartialFunction`.

> For more information, refer to the Scaladoc of the Map trait here: https://www.scala-lang.org/api/current/scala/collection/Map.html.

Mutable and Immutable Collections

So far, we've been covering mostly immutable collections (with the exception of `Iterators`, which are inherently mutable since most operations over it change its state—do note that iterators obtained from the `iterator` method of Scala collections are not expected to mutate the underlying collection). It is important to note, however, that Scala also provides a set of mutable collections in the `scala.collection.mutable` package. Mutable collections provide operations to change the collection in place.

A useful convention for using both immutable and mutable collections in the same place is to import the `scala.collection.mutable` package and prefix collection declaration with the mutable keyword, which is `Map` vs `mutable.Map`.

The following code shows the difference between the immutable and mutable Maps of Scala, showing that the latter has an `update` method that changes the collection in place:

```scala
scala> import scala.collection.mutable
import scala.collection.mutable

scala> val m = Map(1 -> 2, 3 -> 4)
m: scala.collection.immutable.Map[Int,Int] = Map(1 -> 2, 3 -> 4)

scala> val mm = mutable.Map(1 -> 2, 3 -> 4)
mm: scala.collection.mutable.Map[Int,Int] = Map(1 -> 2, 3 -> 4)

scala> mm.update(3, 5)

scala> mm
res1: scala.collection.mutable.Map[Int,Int] = Map(1 -> 2, 3 -> 5)

scala> m.update(3, 5)
<console>:14: error: value update is not a member of scala.collection.
immutable.Map[Int,Int]
       m.update(3, 5)
         ^

scala> m.updated(3, 5)
res3: scala.collection.immutable.Map[Int,Int] = Map(1 -> 2, 3 -> 5)

scala> m
res4: scala.collection.immutable.Map[Int,Int] = Map(1 -> 2, 3 -> 4)
```

Activity: Implementing the Tower of Hanoi Problem

We want to create a solver for the Tower of Hanoi problem. If you are not familiar with the puzzle, visit the Wikipedia page at `https://en.wikipedia.org/wiki/ Tower_of_Hanoi` This is a good entry point for it:

1. Implement the `paths inner` function of the following function:

    ```
    def path(from: Int, to: Int, graph: Map[Int, List[Int]]):
    List[Int] = {
      def paths(from: Int): Stream[List[Int]] = ???
      paths(from).dropWhile(_.head != to).head.reverse
    }
    ```

    The `path` function should return the shortest path from the `from` node to the `to` node in the `graph` graph. The `graph` is defined as an adjacency list encoded as a `Map[Int, List[Int]]`. The path's inner function should return a `Stream` of paths in increasing length (in a breadth-first search manner).

2. Implement the `nextHanoi` function:

    ```
    type HanoiState = (List[Int], List[Int], List[Int])
    def nextHanoi(current: HanoiState): List[HanoiState]
    ```

    The `nextHanoi` function should return a list of valid states one can achieve from the current `HanoiState`. For example: `nextHanoi((List(1, 2, 3), Nil, Nil))` should return `List((List(2, 3),List(1),List()), (List(2, 3),List(),List(1)))`.

3. Generalize the previously implemented path method to be parameterized on the type of state we're operating on:

    ```
    def genericPath[A](from: A, to: A, nextStates: A => List[A]):
    List[A] = {
     def paths(current: A): Stream[List[A]] = ???
      paths(from).dropWhile(_.head != to).head.reverse
    }
    ```

4. With this new implementation, you should be able to solve the Tower of Hanoi problem by calling, for example:

    ```
    val start = (List(1, 2, 3), Nil, Nil)
    val end = (Nil, Nil, List(1, 2, 3))
    genericPath(start, end, nextHanoi)
    ```

5. A possible implementation of the proposed activity is the following:

```
// Does not avoid already visited nodes
def path(from: Int, to: Int, graph: Map[Int, List[Int]]):
List[Int] = {
  def paths(current: Int): Stream[List[Int]] = {
    def bfs(current: Stream[List[Int]]): Stream[List[Int]] = {
      if (current.isEmpty) current
      else current.head #:: bfs(current.tail #::: graph(current.
head.head).map(_ :: current.head).toStream)
    }

    bfs(Stream(List(current)))
  }

  paths(from).dropWhile(_.head != to).head.reverse
}

type HanoiState = (List[Int], List[Int], List[Int])

def nextHanoi(current: HanoiState): List[HanoiState] = {
  def setPile(state: HanoiState, i: Int, newPile: List[Int]):
HanoiState = i match {
...

...
  genericPath(start, end, nextHanoi).size
```

Summary

In this chapter, we covered the Scala Collection library. We covered how to work with lists, which will make us familiar with some design principles of the whole collections library. We also covered how to generalize to sequences and covered some more relevant data structures. Finally, we also covered how collections relate to monads and how we can use that knowledge to use some powerful abstractions in our code.

In the next chapter, we will cover the `type` system and polymorphism. We will also cover the different types of variance, which provides a way to constrain parameterized types. Finally, we will cover some advanced `types` like abstract type members, option, and so on.

5
Scala Type System

In the previous chapter, we covered how to work with lists, which made us familiar with some design principles of the whole collections library. We also covered how to generalize to sequences and covered some more relevant data structures. Finally, we also covered how collections relate to monads and how we can use that knowledge to use some powerful abstractions in our code.

In this chapter, we will cover the `type` system and polymorphism. We will also cover the different types of variance, which provides a way to constrain parameterized types. Finally, we will cover some advanced `types` such as abstract type members, option, and so on.

Scala is statically typed. This means that the type of variables are known at compile time. The main advantage of statically typed languages is that a lot of checks can be done by the compiler, thus increasing the number of trivial bugs that are caught at an early stage. Statically typed languages are also friendlier to refactoring, as the programmer can feel safer about their changes as long as the code compiles.

However, Scala is more than statically typed. In this chapter, we will see how Scala's expressive type system enables and enforces statically typed sound abstractions. The ability to infer types reduces the programmers' workload of annotating the program with redundant type information. This chapter will build upon the fundamentals required for the next chapter, where will be talking about type classes and a type of polymorphism they enable: ad hoc polymorphism.

By the end of this chapter, you will be able to:

- Identify the Scala type hierarchy
- Use the features the Scala type system provides
- Identify abstractions that the Scala type system enables

Type Basics and Polymorphism

In this section, we'll look at different types and polymorphism. We'll start with the unified type system of Scala and end with existential types.

A Unified Type System

Scala has a unified type system. What this means is that all types, including "primitive" types, inherit from a common type. Any is a supertype of all types. It is often called the top type, and defines universal methods such as equals, hashCode, and toString. Nothing is a subtype of all types, and is often called the bottom type. There is no value that has a type of Nothing, so a common use case for it is to signal non-termination: a thrown exception, a program exit, or an infinite loop.

Any has two direct subclasses: AnyVal and AnyRef. Value types are represented by AnyVal. AnyRef represents the reference types. There are nine non-nullable predefined value types: Double, Float, Long, Boolean, Unit, Byte, Char, Short, and Int. All of these types are similar in other programming languages, except Unit. There is one instance of Unit, which is declared like (). Unit is an important return type as all the functions in Scala must return something. All non-value types are defined as reference types. Every user-defined type in Scala is a subtype of AnyRef. Comparing AnyRef to a Java runtime environment, AnyRef is similar to java.lang.Object.

Null is a subtype of all reference types. It contains a single value identified by the literal null. Null is used for operating between other programming languages but it is not recommended to use it in Scala. Scala provides other safer options to null, which we shall cover later in the chapter.

Parametric Polymorphism

Parametric polymorphism is what allows you to write generic code for values of different types without losing the advantages of static typing.

Without polymorphism, a generic list type structure would always look like this:

```
scala> 2 :: 1 :: "bar" :: "foo" :: Nil
res0: List[Any] = List(2, 1, bar, foo)
```

Having to deal with the `Any` type in these cases means that we can't recover any type information about the individual members:

```scala
scala> res0.head
res1: Any = 2
```

Without polymorphism, we would be forced to use casts and thus would lack type safety (since casts are dynamic and happen at runtime).

Scala enables polymorphism through the specification of `type` variables, which you probably already came across when implementing generic functions:

```scala
scala> def drop1[A](l: List[A]) = l.tail
drop1: [A](l: List[A])List[A]

scala> drop1(List(1, 2, 3))
res1: List[Int] = List(2, 3)
```

Type Inference

A common problem of statically typed languages is that they provide too much "syntactic overhead". Scala rectifies this issue by introducing type interface. In Scala, type inference is local and it will consider one expression at a time.

Type inference reduces the need for most type annotations. For example, declaring the type of variable is not necessary in Scala, as the compiler can identify the type from the initialization expression. Return types of methods are also successfully identified by the compiler, as they resemble to the body type:

```scala
val x = 3 + 4 * 5       // the type of x is Int
val y = x.toString()    // the type of y is String
def succ(x: Int) = x + 2  // method succ returns Int values
```

The compiler is not able to infer a result type from recursive methods, though. The following declaration will not compile:

```scala
def fac(n: Int) = if (n == 0) 1 else n * fac(n - 1)
```

The error message is enough to identify the issue:

```
<console>:11: error: recursive method fac needs result type
       def fac(n: Int) = if (n == 0) 1 else n * fac(n - 1)
```

Parameterized Types

Parameterized types are the same as generic types in Java. A generic type is a generic class or interface that is parameterized over types. For example:

```
class Stack[T] {
  var elems: List[T] = Nil
  def push(x: T) { elems = x :: elems }
  def top: T = elems.head
  def pop() {elems = elems.tail }
}
```

Generic types can interact with type checking using bounds or variance. We'll cover variance in the next section.

Bounds

Scala allows programmers to restrict polymorphic variables using bounds. These bounds express subtype (`<:`) or supertype (`:>`) relationships. For example, if we've defined our `drop1` method before as the following:

```
scala> def drop1[A <: AnyRef](l: List[A]) = l.tail
drop1: [A <: AnyRef](l: List[A])List[A]
```

The following wouldn't compile:

```
scala> drop1(List(1, 2, 3))
<console>:13: error: inferred type arguments [Int] do not conform to
method drop1's type parameter bounds [A <: AnyRef]
       drop1(List(1, 2, 3))
       ^
<console>:13: error: type mismatch;
 found   : List[Int]
 required: List[A]
       drop1(List(1, 2, 3))
```

Existential Types

An existential type in Scala is a type with some unknown parts in it. For example:

```
Foo[T] forSome { type T }
```

An existential type includes references to type members that we know exist, but whose concrete values we don't care about. In the preceding code, `T` is a type we don't know concretely, but that we know exists. Using existential types, we can leave some parts of your program unknown, and still typecheck it with different implementations for those unknown parts.

Imagine that you have the following method:

```
scala> def foo(x: Array[Any]) = x.length
foo: (x: Array[Any])Int
```

If you try the following, it won't compile, because an `Array[String]` is not an `Array[Any]` (will see why in the next section):

```
scala> val a = Array("foo", "bar", "baz")
a: Array[String] = Array(foo, bar, baz)

scala> foo(a)
<console>:14: error: type mismatch;
 found    : Array[String]
 required: Array[Any]
We can fix this by adding a type parameter:
scala> def foo[T](x: Array[T]) = x.length
foo: [T](x: Array[T])Int
scala> foo(a)
res0: Int = 3
```

Now, `foo` is parameterized to accept any `T`. But now we have to carry around this `type` parameter, and we only care about methods on `Array` and not what the `Array` contains. We can therefore use existential types to get around this.

```
scala> def foo(x: Array[T] forSome { type T }) = x.length
foo: (x: Array[_])Int

scala> foo(a)
res0: Int = 3
```

This pattern is common, so Scala provides us with "wildcards" for when we don't want to name a type variable:

```
scala> def foo(x: Array[_]) = x.length
foo: (x: Array[_])Int

scala> foo(a)
res0: Int = 3
```

Activity: Generalizing the Implementation of the Binary Tree

In this activity, we'll be generalizing an implementation of a binary search tree. Let's assume you have the following definition for a binary search tree of integers. We want to generalize our implementation of a binary search tree from an `IntTree` to a `Tree[A]`. Perform the necessary modifications to the code to support the new definition and also have the `insert` and `search` methods work on the new definition. You may need to modify the `insert` and `search` definitions to provide a generic comparison function. We would like to use this new generic data structure to store information about the users that visit our website, which are being modeled as the `User(username: String, country: String)` case class:

```scala
trait IntTree
case class IntNode(value: Int, left: IntTree, right: IntTree) extends
IntTree
case object IntEmpty extends IntTree
```

The previous definition supports these methods:

```scala
def insert(value: Int, tree: IntTree): IntTree =
  tree match {
    case IntEmpty => IntNode(value, IntEmpty, IntEmpty)
    case IntNode(currentValue, left, right) =>
      if (value < currentValue)
        IntNode(currentValue, insert(value, left), right)
      else
        IntNode(currentValue, left, insert(value, right))
  }

def search(value: Int, tree: IntTree): Boolean =
  tree match {
    case IntEmpty => false
    case IntNode(currentValue, left, right) =>
      value == currentValue ||
        (value < currentValue && search(value, left)) ||
        (value >= currentValue && search(value, right))
  }
```

1. Start by modifying the ADT for trees from `IntTree` to a `Tree[A]`. Perform the necessary modifications to `IntNode` (to become Node[A] and `IntEmpty` to become `Empty`).

 Note that `IntEmpty` is an object, so there's a single instance for the type `IntEmpty.type`. What should `Empty` be a subtype of? For now, transform `Empty` into a case class: case class `Empty[A]` `()` `extends` `Tree[A]`. We'll look at a better way to define this type later.

2. Modify the `insert` definition to accept an extra comparison function as a function parameter:

   `insert[A](value: A, tree: Tree[A], comp: (A, A) => Boolean).`

3. Modify the code accordingly to take the new `comp` parameter into account.

4. Modify the `search` definition to accept an extra `comparison` function as a function parameter:

   `search[A](value: A, tree: Tree[A], comp: (A, A) => Boolean)`

5. Modify the code accordingly to take the new `comp` parameter into account.

6. Create a comparison function for `User` and use it to populate a `Tree[User]`.

7. Implement the `def usersOfCountry(country: String, tree: Tree[User]): Int` function that returns the number of users of a given country in a `Tree[User]`.

In this section, we covered the unified type system of Scala and how Scala achieves polymorphism. We also introduced type inference and the basic rules of when it's applied. Bounds were also introduced as a convenient way to restrict polymorphic types.

Variance

Variance provides a way to constrain parameterized types. It defines a subtyping relationship between parameterized types based on the subtyping relationship of their component types.

Imagine that you have the following class hierarchy:

```
class Tool
class HandTool extends Tool
class PowerTool extends Tool
class Hammer extends HandTool
class Screwdriver extends HandTool
class Driller extends PowerTool
If we define a generic box:
trait Box[T] {
  def get: T
}
```

How can `Box` of `Tools` relate to one another? Scala provides three ways:

- Covariant: `Box[Hammer] <: Box[Tool]` if `Hammer <: Tool`

- Contravariant: `Box[Tool] <: Box[Hammer]` if `Tool <: Hammer`

- Invariant: There's no subtyping relationship between `Box[Tool]` and `Box[Hammer]` independently of the subtyping relationship of `Tool` and `Hammer`

Covariance

Let's assume that we want to define a function called `isSuitable`, which takes a `Box[HandTool]` and tests if the box is suitable to accommodate the tool it attempts to box:

```
def isSuitable(box: Box[HandTool]) = ???
```

Can you pass a box of hammers to the function? After all, a hammer is a `HandTool`, so if the function wants to determine the suitability of the box based on the underlying tool, it should accept a `Box[Hammer]`. However, if you run the code as it is, you'll get a compilation error:

```
<console>:14: error: type mismatch;
 found    : Box[Hammer]
 required: Box[HandTool]
```

The problem here is that `Box[Hammer]` is not a subtype of `Box[HandTool]`, despite `Hammer` being a subtype of `HandTool`. In this case, we want `Box[B]` to be a subtype of `Box[A]` if `B` is a subtype of `A`. This is what covariance is. We can then tell the Scala compiler that `Box[A]` is a covariant on `A` as:

```
trait Box[+T] {
  def get: T
}
```

Contravariance

Now, let's assume that we have operators that specialize on specific tools, so you have something like this:

```
trait Operator[A] {
  def operate(t: A)
}
```

You have a problem which requires an operator to be capable of working with hammers:

```
def fix(operator: Operator[Hammer]) = ???
```

Can you pass an operator of `HandTool` to fix this? After all, a hammer is a `HandTool`, so if the operator is capable of working with hand tools, they should be able to work with hammers.

However, if you try the code, you get a compilation error:

```
<console>:14: error: type mismatch;
 found    : Operator[HandTool]
 required: Operator[Hammer]
```

The problem here is that `Operator[HandTool]` is not a subtype of `Operator[Hammer]`, despite `Hammer` being a subtype of `HandTool`. In this case, we want `Operator[A]` to be a subtype of `Operator[B]` if `B` is a subtype of `A`. This is what contravariance is. We can tell the Scala compiler that `Operator[A]` is a contravariant on `A` as:

```
trait Operator[-A] {
  def operate(t: A)
}
```

Invariance

By default, type parameters are invariant because the compiler has no way of guessing what you intend to model with a given type. On the other hand, the compiler helps you by forbidding the definition of types that may be unsound. For example, if you declare the `Operator` class as a covariant, you get a compilation error:

```
scala> trait Operator[+A] { def operate(t: A) }
<console>:11: error: covariant type A occurs in contravariant position
in type A of value t
       trait Operator[+A] { def operate(t: A) }
```

By defining `Operator` to be covariant, you would say that an `Operator [Hammer]` could be used in place of an `Operator [HandTool]`. So, an operator capable of only using a `Hammer` would be able to operate on any `HandTool`.

Looking at the definitions of `Box [+A]` and `Operator [-A]`, notice that type `A` only appears in the return type of methods of `Box [+A]` and only in the parameters of methods of `Operator [-A]`. So, a type that only produces values of type `A` can be made covariant on `A`, and a type that consumes values of type `A` can be made contravariant on `A`.

You can deduce by the previous points that mutable data types are necessarily invariant (they have `getters` and `setters`, so they both produce and consume values).

In fact, Java has an issue with this, as Java arrays are covariant. This means that some code that is valid at compile time can fail at runtime. For example:

```
String[] strings = new String[1];
Object[] objects = strings;
objects[0] = new Integer(1); // RUN-TIME FAILURE
```

In Scala, most collections are covariant (for example, `List [+A]`). However, you may be wondering how the `::` methods and similar are implemented, since they may have a type in a contravariant position:

```
trait List[+A] {
  def ::(a: A): List[A]
}
```

Actually, methods such as `::` are implemented as follows:

```
def ::[B >: A](a: B): List[B]
```

This actually allows collections to always get parameterized on the more specific type they're able to. Notice how the following list gets lifted to a list of `HandTool`:

```
scala> val l = List(new Hammer {}, new Hammer {}, new Hammer {})
l: List[Hammer] = List($anon$1@79dd6dfe, $anon$2@2f478dcf,
$anon$3@3b88adb0)

scala> val l2 = new Screwdriver {} :: l
l2: List[HandTool] = List($anon$1@7065daac, $anon$1@79dd6dfe,
$anon$2@2f478dcf, $anon$3@3b88adb0)
```

Activity: Implementing Covariance and the Database for Tools

In this activity, we'll be making our previous implementation of Tree[A] covariant on A. We also want to start building a database for the tools we've defined so far. We have extended the definition of tools to now have a weight and a price:

```
trait Tool {
  def weight: Long
  def price: Long
}

trait HandTool extends Tool
trait PowerTool extends Tool
case class Hammer(weight: Long, price: Long) extends HandTool
case class Screwdriver(weight: Long, price: Long) extends HandTool
case class Driller(weight: Long, price: Long) extends PowerTool
```

1. Start by defining Tree as Tree[+A]. You can now define Empty as a case object extending Tree[Nothing].

2. Define some comparison function for tools. For instance, you can compare tools by weight, by price, or by a combination of both. Experiment with the different comparison functions when creating trees.

3. Implement the def merge[A](tree1: Tree[A], tree2: Tree[A], comp: (A, A) => Boolean): Tree[A] function, which merges two trees into one.

In this section, we've covered variance as a way to define subtyping relationships on types based on their component types.

Advanced Types

If you have come from Java, most of these things may not be surprising. As such, let's look at some other features of Scala's type system.

Abstract Type Members

Abstract type members are type members of an object or class that are left abstract. They can provide some abstraction without the verbosity of type parameters. If a type is intended to be used existentially in most cases, we can cut some verbosity by using a type member instead of a parameter.

```
class Operator {
  type ToolOfChoice
}
```

```scala
class Susan extends Operator {
  type ToolOfChoice = Hammer
}


class Operator[ToolOfChoice]
class Susan extends Operator[ToolOfChoice]
```

You can refer to an abstract type variable using the hash operator:

```scala
scala> val tool: Susan#ToolOfChoice = new Hammer
tool: Hammer = Hammer@d8756ac
```

Structural Types

Scala supports structural types: type requirements that are expressed by an interface structure instead of a concrete type. Structural typing provides a feature similar to what dynamic languages allow you to do when they support duck typing, but in a static typed implementation checked up at compile time. However, bear in mind that Scala uses reflection to call methods on structural types, and that this has a cost on performance:

```scala
def quacker(duck: { def quack(value: String): String }) {
  println(duck.quack("Quack"))
}

object BigDuck {
  def quack(value: String) = value.toUpperCase
}

object SmallDuck {
  def quack(value: String) = value.toLowerCase
}
...
...
 required: AnyRef{def quack(value: String): String}
       quacker(NotADuck)
```

Structural types are not very common in Scala codebases.

Option

We previously visited the `Null` type in the Scala hierarchy, but commented that null is rarely seen in Scala code. The reason behind this is the existence of the `Option` type in Scala's standard library. If you have worked with Java in the past, chances are you came across a `NullPointerException` at some point. That usually happens when some method returns `null` when the programmer was not expecting it to and not dealing with that possibility in the client code. Scala tries to solve the problem by making optional types explicit via the `Option[A]` trait. `Option[A]` is a container for an optional value of type `A`. If the value is present, then `Option[A]` is an instance of `Some[A]`, otherwise it is the `None` object. By making optional values explicit at the type level, there's no way to accidentally rely on the presence of a value that is really optional.

You can create an `Option` using the `Some` case class or by assigning the `None` object. When working with Java libraries, you can use the factory method of the `Option` companion object that creates `None` if the given parameter is null, and wraps the parameter in a `Some` otherwise:

```
val intOption1: Option[Int] = Some(2)
val intOption2: Option[Int] = None
val strOption: Option[String] = Option(null)
```

The `Option` trait defines a get method that returns the wrapped value in case of a Some, and throws a `NoSuchElementException` in case of a `None`. A safer method is `getOrElse`, which returns the wrapped value in case of a Some, but a default value in case of a None. Do note that the default value in the `getOrElse` method is a by-name-parameter, so it will only be evaluated in case of a `None`.

A convenient way to work with Options is by using pattern matching:

```
def foo(v: Option[Int]) = v match {
  case Some(value) => println(s"I have a value and it's $value.")
  case None => println("I have no value.")
}
```

A nice feature of `Option` is that it extends `Traversable`, so you have all the `map`, `flatMap`, `fold`, `reduce`, and other methods we visited in the previous chapter.

Higher Kind Types

Scala can abstract over types of a higher kind. You can think of it as types of types. A common use case for it is if you want to abstract over several types of containers for several types of data. You may want to define an interface for these containers without nailing down the value's type:

```
trait Container[M[_]] {
  def put[A](x: A): M[A]
  def get[A](m: M[A]): A
}

val listContainer = new Container[List] {
  def put[A](x: A) = List(x)
  def get[A](m: List[A]) = m.head
}

scala> listContainer.put("str")
res0: List[String] = List(str)

scala> listContainer.put(123)
res1: List[Int] = List(123)
```

Type Erasure

To incur in no runtime overhead, the Java Virtual Machine performs type erasure. Among other things, type erasure replaces all type parameters in generic types with their bounds or Object if the type parameters are unbounded. This results in bytecode that only contains ordinary classes, interfaces, and methods, and makes sure that no new classes are created for parameterized types. This leads to some pitfalls when we attempt to match on generic type parameters:

```
def optMatch[A](opt: Any) = opt match {
  case opt: Option[Int] => println(s"Got Option[Int]: $opt.")
  case opt: Option[String] => println(s"Got Option[String]: $opt.")
  case other => println(s"Got something else: $other.")
}

scala> optMatch(Some(123))
Got Option[Int]: Some(123).

scala> optMatch(Some("str"))
Got Option[Int]: Some(str).
```

As such, you should always avoid matching on generic type parameters. If it is impossible to refactor the method that performs the pattern matching, try to control the type of value passed into the function by boxing the input which has a type parameter with a container that specifies the type parameter:

```
case class IntOption(v: Option[Int])
case class StringOption(v: Option[String])
```

Activity: Finding an Element Based on a Given Predicate

In this activity, we want to provide our `Tree` with functionality to find an element in it based on a given predicate. More concretely, we want to implement the `def find[A](tree: Tree[A], predicate: A => Boolean): Option[A]` function. The function should return `None` if no element is found that satisfies the predicate, or `Some` with the first element (in order) that satisfies it.

1. We want to return the first element in order, so we need to assume that the tree is a search tree and traverse it in order. Implement the `def inOrder[A] (tree: Tree[A]): Iterator[A]` method that returns an `Iterator` with the in-order traversal of elements in the `Tree`.

2. Using the previously implemented method, now rely on the `find` method of `Iterator` to implement the `target` function.

3. We want to find the cheapest tool with a weight below 100. Implement the function that should be used when creating the tree, and the predicate to be used in the `find` method.

Summary

In this chapter, we covered the `type` system and polymorphism. We also covered the different types of variance which provide a way to constrain parameterized types. Finally, we covered some advanced `types` such as abstract type members, option, and so on.

In the next chapter, we will cover `implicits`, which will make working with external libraries more pleasant. We will cover implicit conversions and finally cover ad hoc polymorphism through the use of type classes.

6
Implicits

In the previous chapter, we covered the `type` system and polymorphism. We also covered the different types of variance which provide ways to constrain parameterized types. Finally, we covered some advanced `types` such as abstract type members, option, and so on.

In this chapter, we will cover implicit parameters and implicit conversions. We'll be learning about how they work, how to use them, and what kind of benefits and perils they provide.

When using a third-party library in your code, you usually have to take its code as it is. This can make some libraries unpleasant to deal with. It can be either the code style that differs from the one in your code base or simply some functionality that the library lacks that you can't elegantly supply.

Some languages have come up with solutions to alleviate this problem. Ruby has modules, Smalltalk allows packages to add to each other's classes, and C# 3.0 has static extension methods.

Scala has implicit parameters and conversions. When used in a controlled manner, implicits can make working with external libraries more pleasant, and also enable some elegant patterns that you can use in your own code.

By the end of this chapter, you will be able to:

- Describe implicits and how the Scala compiler handles them
- Explain the design patterns that implicits enable
- Analyze the common issues that may arise by overusing implicits

Implicit Parameters and Implicit Conversions

Scala has implicit parameters and conversions. When used in a controlled manner, implicit can make working with external libraries more pleasant, and also enable some elegant patterns that you can use in your own code.

Implicit Parameters

Implicit parameters are a way to make the compiler automatically fill in some arguments when a method call misses them for some (or all) of the (implicit) parameters. The compiler will look for definitions labelled implicit of the required types. For example, suppose you want to write a program that prompts the user for some action, after displaying a message. You want to customize both the message and the string that appear on the prompt. We can assume that the prompt string will have a more default value than the message, so one way to implement it using implicit parameters is like the following:

```
case class Prompt(value: String)
def message(msg: String)(implicit prompt: Prompt) = {
  println(msg)
  println(s"${prompt.value}>")
}
```

With the previous implementation, you can call the message function, supplying an argument to the prompt parameter explicitly:

```
message("Welcome!")(Prompt("action"))
```

However, if we want to reuse the prompt in different message calls, we can create a default object.

default:

```
object Defaults {
  implicit val defaultPrompt = Prompt("action")
}
```

We can then bring that `default` into scope when we use the message method and avoid having to explicitly supply the prompt parameter:

```
import Defaults._
message("Welcome!")
message("What do you want to do next?")
```

There can be only one implicit parameter list per method, but it can have multiple parameters. The implicit parameter list must be the last parameter list of the function.

The eligible arguments for an implicit parameter are identifiers that can be accessed at the point of the method call without a prefix and that denote an implicit definition or an implicit parameter, and members of companion modules of the implicit parameter's type that are labelled implicit. For example, in the previous example, if you were to put the `defaultPrompt` implicit in the companion object of `Prompt`, it wouldn't be necessary to import `Prompt` to put `defaultPrompt` into scope on calls to message:

```
object Prompt {
   implicit val defaultPrompt = Prompt("action")
}
message("Welcome!")
message("What do you want to do next?")
```

Implicit Conversions

Implicit conversions provide a way to transparently convert between `types`. Implicit conversions are useful when you need a `type` that you don't control (from an external library, for example) to adhere to a specified interface. For example, suppose you want to handle an integer as a traversable, so you can iterate through its digits. One way to do this is by supplying an implicit conversion:

```
implicit def intToIterable(i: Int): Traversable[Int] =
  new Traversable[Int] {
  override def foreach[U](f: Int => U): Unit = {
    var value = i
    var l = List.empty[Int]
    do {
      l = value % 10 :: l
      value /= 10
    } while (value != 0)
    l.foreach(f)
  }
}
```

The `intToIterable` implicit conversion works as a normal method. The special thing is the implicit keyword at the start of the definition. You can still apply the conversion explicitly or leave it out and get the same behavior:

```
scala> intToIterable(123).size
res0: Int = 3
scala> 123.size
res1: Int = 3
scala> 123 ++ 456
res2: Traversable[Int] = List(1, 2, 3, 4, 5, 6)
```

The best thing about implicit conversions is that they support conversions for a type that's needed at some point in the code. For example, if you have the following function, which returns an ordered Seq from a Traversable:

```
def orderedSeq[A: Ordering](t: Traversable[A]) = t.toSeq.sorted
```

 You can pass an Int to orderedSeq, since there's an implicit conversion from Int to Traversable[Int].

```
orderedSeq(472).toList
// Returns List(2, 4, 7)
```

When used indiscriminately, implicits can be dangerous, as they can enable runtime errors in locations where we would preferably want the compiler to not compile the code.

You should avoid implicit conversions between common types. The Scala compiler signals implicit conversions as dangerous by warning when you define one by default.

As seen before, implicit conversions enable syntax-like extensions to the language. The pattern is common throughout the standard library and libraries in the Scala ecosystem. The pattern is usually called "rich wrappers", so when you see a class named RichFoo, it is likely that it is adding syntax-like extensions to the Foo type.

To provide allocation-free extension methods, you can use implicit classes combined with value classes. For example, if you have the following RichInt definition:

```
implicit class RichInt(val self: Int) extends AnyVal {
  def toHexString: String = java.lang.Integer.toHexString(self)
}
```

A call to 3.toHexString, for example, will result in a method call in a static object (RichInt$.MODULE$.extension$toHexString(3)) rather than a method call on a newly instantiated one.

Implicit Resolution

It is important to know where the compiler looks for implicits and, even more importantly, how it decides which implicit to use in situations of apparent ambiguity.

For more information on implicit resolution, refer to: `https://docs.scala-lang.org/tutorials/FAQ/ finding-implicits.html`.

For choosing the most specific implicit definition based on the rules of static overloading resolution, refer to: `http://scala-lang.org/files/archive/ spec/2.11/06-expressions.html`.

The rules of implicit resolution are a bit challenging to remember, so experimenting with them can give you more intuition over the Scala compiler.

The following list defines where the compiler looks for implicits:

- Implicits which are defined in the current scope
- Explicit Imports
- Wildcard Imports
- Companion Objects of Type
- Implicit Scope of an Argument's Type
- Implicit Scope of Type Arguments
- Outer Objects for Nested Types

Activity: Creation of Extension Methods

In this activity, we'll be creating extension methods for the `Int` type by relying on implicit conversions.

1. Start by defining a new class, `RichInt`, which will implement your desired methods.
2. Create an implicit conversion from `Int` to `RichInt`. You can either create an implicit method or an implicit value class. Since it's important to avoid the runtime overhead, an implicit value class is advisable.
3. Implement the methods `square` and `plus`.
4. Make sure the implicit conversion is in scope, and experiment with calling `square` and `plus` on values of type `Int`.

This section covered implicit parameters and implicit conversions. We saw how to enable elegant extension methods for your code. We also had a look at how the Scala compiler resolves implicits.

Ad Hoc Polymorphism and Type Classes

In this section, we'll be exploring ad hoc polymorphism, but through the usage of type classes.

Types of Polymorphism

In computer science, polymorphism is the provision of a single interface to entities of different types. Polymorphism consists of three types: subtyping, parametric polymorphism, and ad hoc polymorphism.

Subtyping enables polymorphism by having different implementations of the same method (but keeping the interface) in the different subclasses. Parametric polymorphism enables polymorphism by allowing code to be written without the mention of a specific type. For example, when you operate over a generic List, you're applying parametric polymorphism. Ad hoc polymorphism enables polymorphism by allowing different and heterogeneous implementations depending on specified types. Method overloading is an example of ad hoc polymorphism.

Type Classes

Type classes are a construct that enable ad hoc polymorphism. They originally appeared in Haskell, which has native support for them, but transitioned to Scala through the use of implicits.

At its core, a type class is a class with a type parameter that aims to bridge type hierarchies. That is, we want to provide behavior to a type hierarchy by parameterizing our type class and providing specific implementations for concrete types. Type classes provide an easy way to extend libraries without touching existing code.

As a running example throughout this section, consider the following implementation of JSON:

```
sealed trait JsValue
case class JsObject(fields: Map[String, JsValue]) extends JsValue
case class JsArray(elements: Vector[JsValue]) extends JsValue
case class JsString(value: String) extends JsValue
case class JsNumber(value: BigDecimal) extends JsValue

sealed trait JsBoolean extends JsValue
case object JsTrue extends JsBoolean
case object JsFalse extends JsBoolean

case object JsNull extends JsValue
```

We will be introducing a type class called `JsonWriter[A]`, whose interface has a single method `write`, which, given an `A`, returns a `JsValue`. Let's define `JsonWriter` and provide two implementations of it, one for `Int` and another for `String`:

```
trait JsonWriter[A] {
  def write(value: A): JsValue
}

object JsonWriter {
  implicit object IntJsonWriter extends JsonWriter[Int] {
    def write(value: Int): JsValue = JsNumber(value)
  }

  implicit object StringJsonWriter extends JsonWriter[String] {
    def write(value: String): JsValue = JsString(value)
  }
}
```

We can use these specific implementations of `JsonWriter` to convert `Int`s and `Strings` to JSON. For example, we can call `IntJsonWriter.write(4)` and `StringJsonWriter.write("Hello World")`. However, we don't want to be calling writers explicitly.

Instead of calling `JsonWriters` explicitly, we introduce the `toJson` method, which is capable of converting a type to JSON, provided that there is a `JsonWriter` in the scope:

```
def toJson[A](value: A)(implicit jw: JsonWriter[A]) =
  jw.write(value)
```

We have now introduced ad hoc polymorphism in the `toJson` function. Based on the type of value provided to `toJson`, we have different behaviors for the `toJson` function, controlled by the `JsonWriters` available in scope. The matter of scope is important. Recall that there is precedence to the implicit resolution. As such, library authors can provide their own default implementations for their type classes, but you can always override it in your client code while keeping the same interface.

Context Bounds and Implicitly

Context bounds are syntactic sugar that reduce verbosity when you need to pass implicits around. By using a context bound, you reduce the need of an implicit parameter list. However, when using a context bound, you lose access to the implicit argument used when calling the method. To provide access to it, you can use the `implicitly` function. Implicitly provides access to the implicit of the requested type in scope. Its implementation is simply this:

```
def implicitly[T](implicit e: T) = e
```

Type Classes in the Standard Library

The type class pattern is heavily used in the Scala standard library. Prime examples of its usage are the `Ordering` type classes previously introduced and the `CanBuildFrom` type class, which represents builder factories for Scala collections.

 Please take a look at the `Ordering` and `CanBuildFrom` type classes on your own. A good overview of the `CanBuildFrom` type class can be obtained from the following guide: `http://docs.scala-lang.org/ overviews/core/architecture-of-scala-collections.html`.

Activity: Implementing Type Classes to Support Conversion

In this activity, we'll be implementing `type` classes to support conversions to `JsValue` for common Scala types. Consider the `JsValue` ADT that was introduced in the beginning of the section.

1. Start by defining, if you haven't already, the `toJson` method:

   ```
   def toJson[A](value: A)(implicit jw: JsonWriter[A]): JsValue and
   the JsonWriter trait as trait JsonWriter[A] { def write(value: A):
   JsValue }
   ```

2. Implement `JsonWriter` for `Int`, `String`, and `Boolean`. The implementation for `Int` and `String` was already provided. A good place to put those implementations, according to the implicit resolution rules previously introduced, is in the companion object of `JsonWriter`.

3. Implement `JsonWriter` for `List`, `Set`, and `Map`. In these generic collections, note that you can provide a `JsonWriter[List[A]]`, for example, if you have a `JsonWriter` for `A`. Not all maps are convertible to JSON, so only provide a `JsonWriter[Map[String, A]]`.

Summary

In this chapter, we covered implicit parameters and implicit conversions. We saw how to enable elegant extension methods for your code. We also had a look at how the Scala compiler resolves implicits. Finally, we covered how implicits work, how to use them, and what kind of benefits they provide.

In the next chapter, we'll cover the core concepts of functional programming such as Pure functions, immutability, and higher-order functions. We'll build upon this understanding and introduce some of the design patterns that are prevalent in large functional programs that you'll no doubt run into once you start to use Scala libraries that focus on functional programming. Finally, we'll cover two popular functional programming libraries called `Cats` and `Doobie`, and use them to write some interesting programs.

7
Functional Idioms

In the previous chapter, we covered implicit parameters and implicit conversions. We saw how to enable elegant extension methods for your code. We also had a look at how the Scala compiler resolves implicits. Finally, we covered how implicits work, how to use them, and what kind of benefits they provide.

In this chapter, we'll cover the core concepts of functional programming like `Pure` functions, immutability, and higher-order functions. We'll build upon this understanding and introduce some of the design patterns that are prevalent in large functional programs that you'll no doubt run into once you start to use Scala libraries that focus on functional programming. Finally, we'll cover two popular functional programming libraries called `Cats` and `Doobie`, and use them to write some interesting programs.

Functional programming languages have been around for a very long time, but they have gotten more traction lately, with functional programming concepts being adopted by most popular programming languages. A reason for this might be that functional programming lends itself easily to solving some problems that are hard in imperative languages, such as writing parallelizable programs. Functional programming can also increase the modularity of your programs and thus make them easier to test, reuse, and reason about, hopefully resulting in code that produces fewer bugs.

By the end of this chapter, you will be able to:

- Identify the core concepts of functional programming
- Recognize and implement the popular functional programming design patterns
- Implement Cats and Doobie in your own Scala projects

Introduction to Functional Programming Concepts

In this section, we will cover the core concepts behind functional programming and give you the necessary knowledge to understand and write simple functional programs.

By the end of this section, you should have a good understanding of the core concepts behind functional programming, such as:

- Writing and using pure functions
- Using immutable classes instead of mutable classes
- Writing and using higher-order functions

Pure Functions

At the very core of functional programming is the concept of a `pure` function. A function is pure if it doesn't have any side effects, that is, the function simply computes a result based on the arguments to the function and does nothing else.

Examples of side effects are modifying variables, setting fields on objects, performing input/output operations such as reading or writing a file, printing values to the console, and many more.

Let's look at some examples of both `pure` and `impure` functions to better understand the difference. Let's have a look at two functions:

```
case class Person(var name: String, var age: Int)

def birthday(p: Person) = p.age += 1

def getName(p: Person) = {
  println(s"Getting the name of ${p.name}")
  p.name
}

def rename(p: Person, name: String) =
  Person(name, p.age)
```

Here, we define a simple case class called `Person` with a `name` and an `age`. Then, we define two functions that operate on `Person`. Can you see why these functions are not pure functions? To test if these functions are pure, we could try to invoke them with the same arguments twice to see if we get different results – remember, a pure function is a function that simply computes a result based on the arguments to the function and does nothing else.

Let's start with `birthday`:

```
val p = Person("Jack", 41)
birthday(p)
println(p) // prints Person(Jack,42)
birthday(p)
println(p) // prints Person(Jack,43)
```

Alright, so `birthday` isn't a pure function as it's modifying the state of the `Person` p passed to the function. We also might have been able to guess this as the return type of birthday is `Unit` – as the function doesn't return a value, it must be doing some side effects, otherwise the function would be completely useless.

Next up, let's take a look at `getName`:

```
val n1 = getName(p) // Getting the name of Jack
val n2 = getName(p) // Getting the name of Jack
println(n1) // Jack
println(n2) // Jack
```

The good news is that the function returns the name value and provides the same arguments. However, the function is still not pure as it prints to the console whenever it's invoked.

Lastly, let's have a look at `rename`:

```
val r1 = rename(p, "John")
val r2 = rename(p, "John")
println(r1) // Person(John,43)
println(r2) // Person(John,43)
```

Alright, so `rename` is a pure function. When provided with the same argument, it produces the same value and doesn't perform any observable side effects.

We have now covered the concept of a pure function and seen examples of both pure and impure functions. You've seen two ways to define what a pure function is:

- When provided with the same argument, it produces the same value and doesn't perform any observable side effects.

- A pure function is a function that only consists of referentially transparent expressions. An expression is referentially transparent if it can be replaced with its value without changing the behavior of the program.

In the next subsection, we'll look at immutability, which is another core concept that enables the writing of pure functions.

Immutability

With the understanding of what a pure function is, it's time to introduce another core concept that enables the writing of pure functions: immutability. Something is said to be immutable if you can't change it – it's the opposite of mutable.

One of the reasons Scala is so well suited for functional programming is that it provides constructs where immutability is guaranteed. Let's look at some examples.

If we define a variable or field on a class using the val keyword (rather than var), then the Scala compiler will not allow us to change that value.

1. Open Terminal on your computer.
2. Start the Scala REPL by typing scala.
3. Now, you can start pasting in the code after scala>:

```
scala> val x = "test"
x: String = test

scala> x = "test 2"
<console>:12: error: reassignment to val
       x = "test 2"
```

4. The expected output is shown on the line below scala>.
5. However, Scala can't guarantee that you don't modify the state of the value that was assigned to a variable, for example:

```
scala> case class Person(var name: String)
defined class Person

scala> val p = Person("Jack")
p: Person = Person(Jack)

scala> p.name
res0: String = Jack
```

```
scala> p.name = "John"
p.name: String = John

scala> p
res1: Person = Person(John)
```

6. However, if we remove the var keyword, Scala will, by default, declare the field name using val and thus won't allow us to change it, thereby enforcing immutability.

Implementing the standard library

The standard library in Scala has a whole collection of immutable data structures in the scala.collection.immutable package.

The most used of these is perhaps scala.collection.immutable.List, which is imported in Predef and thus accessible in Scala programs simply as List:

```
scala> val xs = List(1,2,3)
xs: List[Int] = List(1, 2, 3)

scala> xs.reverse
res0: List[Int] = List(3, 2, 1)
scala> xs
res1: List[Int] = List(1, 2, 3)
```

Here, you can see that xs.reverse returns a new List that is reversed and leaves xs unmodified.

Scala provides constructs where immutability is guaranteed and has many defaults where immutability is used, such as when defining case classes or using some of the immutable collection that is provided by the standard library. In the next subsection, we'll look at higher-order functions, which you'll be using extensively when writing programs in Scala using functional programming.

Higher-Order Functions

Higher-order functions are functions that take other functions as arguments. This is a technique that is widely used in Scala, and one that you will use all the time when you're writing Scala programs. Higher-order functions have already been covered previously, but we will include a short recap here for completeness.

Here's an example of using the higher-order function map on `List` to invoke a function on every item of the list to produce a new `List`:

```scala
scala> val xs = List(1,2,3,4,5)
xs: List[Int] = List(1, 2, 3, 4, 5)

scala> xs.map(_ * 2)
res0: List[Int] = List(2, 4, 6, 8, 10)
```

Note that this example uses pure functions, immutability, and higher-order functions – the perfect functional program.

Here's an example of how to define a higher-order function. It takes a function from `A => Boolean` and returns a function of `A => Boolean` that negates the result of the original function:

```scala
def negate[A](f: A => Boolean): A => Boolean =
  (a: A) => !f(a)
```

We'll write a higher-order function that finds the second element in a list given a predicate:

```scala
def sndWhere[A](xs: List[A])(pred: A => Boolean): Option[A] = ???
```

Here are two examples of using the function:

```scala
println(sndWhere(List(1,3,2,4,4))(_ > 2)) // Some(4)
println(sndWhere(List(1,3,2,4,4))(_ > 10)) // None
```

Now, try to write your own higher-order function to get a better feeling for how they work.

1. Create a new Scala file in your editor named `HOExample.scala`.

2. Paste in the following code:

```scala
object HOExample extends App {
  def sndWhere[A](xs: List[A])(pred: A => Boolean): Option[A] =
???
  println(sndWhere(List(1, 3, 2, 4, 4))(_ > 2)) // Some(4)
  println(sndWhere(List(1, 3, 2, 4, 4))(_ > 10)) // None
}
```

3. This higher-order function should find the second element in a list given a predicate.

4. When you run the application in your editor, you should see the following output:

```
Some(4)
None
```

5. One possible solution is:

```
def sndWhere[A](xs: List[A])(pred: A => Boolean): Option[A] =

  xs.filter(pred) match {

    case _ :: snd :: _ => Some(snd)

    case _             => None

  }
```

We've gotten a recap of what higher-order functions are and seen how they can be used to write generic functions where some of the functionality of the function is provided by an argument to the function.

In the next section, we'll move beyond the basic concepts behind functional programming and look at some of the functional design patterns that you'll encounter when using functional libraries.

You've seen three of the cornerstones of functional programming:

- **Pure functions**: A function simply computes a result based on the arguments to the function and does nothing else.

- **Immutability**: You've seen how Scala has good support for immutability and uses it as the default in many cases.

- **Higher-order functions**: Functions that take others as arguments or return a function are called higher-order functions.

Functional Design Patterns

In this section, we are moving beyond the basic concepts behind functional programming and looking at some of the functional design patterns that you'll encounter when using functional libraries. You will be introduced to `Monoids`, `Functors`, `Monads`, and other functional programming patterns that you can use to structure your programs – these patterns are the functional programming equivalent of the object-oriented design patterns that you might be familiar with from when you first learned about OOP.

Have you ever heard of category theory? The patterns we'll see in this section come from category theory. Each concept (such as a `Monoid`) has a clear mathematical definition and set of associated laws.

 In this section, we won't go into detail regarding these laws, but should you want to research this topic further, it's good to know that the field is called category theory.

This will set you up for further study of functional design patterns and enable you to use some of the most popular functional programming libraries such as `Cats` and `Scalaz`.

The following subsections will each introduce an abstract structure, show its definition in Scala, and show how to use it when you write your programs – the structures might seem very abstract at first, but please be patient, as the examples will show you how the structures can be very useful.

 The following code will heavily use type classes, so please refer back to the previous chapters to make sure you have a good understanding of them.

Monoids

The first structure we'll take a look at is called a `Monoid`. A `Monoid` is a very simple structure, but it's one that you'll encounter all the time once you've learned to recognize it.

A `Monoid` has two operations, `combine` and `empty`. In Scala, the definition of a Monoid could be expressed as a type class like the following:

```
trait Monoid[A] {
  def combine(x: A, y: A): A
  def empty: A
}
```

That is, instances of the `Monoid` type class support two operations:

- `combine`: This operation takes two arguments of type `A` and returns an `A`.

- `empty`: This operation doesn't take any arguments but it returns an `A`.

In category theory, these operations are called `multiplication` and `unit`. This might be useful if you want to learn more about this topic at a later date.

This is very abstract, so let's make it concrete by looking at some examples.

Let's look at one of the instances of the `Monoid` type class to get a better feeling for how it works and how you can use it.

1. Define a `Monoid` type class instance for `String`, that is, a `Monoid[String]`:

```
implicit val strMonoid = new Monoid[String] {
  def combine(x: String, y: String): String = x + y
 def empty: String = ""
}
```

2. Define the `stringMonoid` as follows:

```
strMonoid.combine("Monoids are ", "great")
strMonoid.combine("Hello", strMonoid.empty)
```

In most cases, you won't refer to a concrete instance of Monoid as explicitly as we've done here, but rather you'll use the `Monoid` type class when writing polymorphic functions, as you'll see in the example after the exercises.

Let's create implicit def for Monoid creation.

1. Write an instance of `Monoid` for `Int`:

```
implicit val intMonoid = new Monoid[Int] {
    def combine(x: Int, y: Int): Int = x + y
    def empty: Int = 0
  }
```

2. Write an `implicit def` that can create a `Monoid[List[A]]` for any `A`:

```
implicit def listMonoid[A]: Monoid[List[A]] =
  new Monoid[List[A]] {
  def combine(x: List[A], y: List[A]): List[A] = ???
    def empty: List[A] = ???
  }
```

Using Monoids to Write Polymorphic Functions

Even though the Monoid might seem simple, it is immensely useful. The power of Monoid, and the other structures that you'll be introduced to later, come into play when we define polymorphic functions that know nothing about their arguments other than the fact that a Monoid instance for their types exists.

Let's write a function that takes the sum of a list:

```
def sum[A](xs: List[A])(implicit m: Monoid[A]): A =
  xs.foldLeft(m.empty)(m.combine)
```

The first parameter list is straightforward – it defines that the function takes a List of the different A values. However, the second implicit parameter list asks the compiler to find an instance of Monoid for A and will only allow you to invoke sum[A] if an instance of Monoid[A] exists.

With this function, you can take the sum of any List as long as there is an appropriate instance of Monoid in scope:

```
sum(List("Monoids", " are", " cool")) // "Monoids are cool"
sum(List(1,2,3)) // 6
sum(List(List(1,2),List(3,4)) // List(1,2,3,4)
```

We looked at the first structure, the Monoid. We saw that even though the Monoid has a very simple interface, it showed itself to be a useful construct that allowed us to write interesting polymorphic functions. In the next section, we'll look at Functors. Put simply, a Functor is something that you can map over.

Functor

The second structure we'll look at is the Functor. Put simply, a Functor is something that you can map over. In Scala, you'll be very familiar with this operation as you've no doubt used it multiple times to manipulate Lists, Options, and so on. In Scala, the type class for Functors could look something like this:

```
trait Functor[F[_]] {
  def map[A, B](fa: F[A])(f: A => B): F[B]
}
```

 The Functor abstracts over a type constructor, F – types that abstract over type constructors are called higher types.

You might be tempted to think of map as a convenient way to iterate over a collection such as List or Set, but in the context of Functor, there's a more interesting way to look at it. You should think of map as a way of sequencing operations on some type that preserves the structure of the type as defined by the specificities of the type. The details will vary depending on the type:

- **Option**: There might not be a value.

- **List**: There might be zero or more values.

- **Either**: There might be an error or there might be a value – not both.

Let's look at some concrete examples to make this more clear.

Let's now evaluate the same thing in different contexts.

1. Write a polymorphic function that abstracts over different Functors:

```
def compute[F[_]](fa: F[Int])(implicit f: Functor[F]): F[Int] = {
 val fx = f.map(fa) { _ + 2 }
   f.map(fx) { _ * 2}
}
```

It defines a function, compute, that first uses map to add 2 to the value inside the functor and then uses map to multiply the result by 2.

2. We can now invoke this method with any value that has a Functor instance defined:

```
compute(List(1,2,3)) // List(6, 8, 10)
compute(Option(2) // Some(8)
compute(Right(2): Either[String, Int]) // Right(8)
```

With this exercise in mind, you can see how Functor allows you to write polymorphic functions that know nothing about their arguments other than that there's a map function defined for them. It's up to the specific Functor to define what map means in its specific context.

Let's define and use a Functor for List and Option.

1. Define a Functor for List:

```
implicit val listFunctor = new Functor[List] {
   def map[A, B](fa: List[A])(f: A => B): List[B] = fa.map(f)
}
```

2. Using it would then look something like this:

```
listFunctor.map(List(1,2,3))(_ * 2)
```

Defining Functor for Option

1. Write an instance of `Functor` for `Option`:

 The solution can be found in `Examples/src/main/scala/Functor.scala`, defined as `optionFunctor`.

```scala
implicit val optionFunctor = new Functor[Option] {
   def map[A, B](fa: Option[A])(f: A => B): Option[B] = fa match
{
      case None => None
      case Some(x) => Some(f(x))
   }
```

We looked at our second structure, the Functor, which represents things that can be mapped over. You saw how to define instances for Functor and how one can think of map as a way of sequencing operations on some type that preserves the structure of the type, as defined by the specificities of the type. In the next section, we'll look at Monads – a structure that you might already be familiar with without knowing it.

Monads

The last structure we'll look at is the Monad. Most Scala programmers will be familiar with Monads, even if they don't know them by name, as the abstraction is used whenever you write a for-comprehension. A Monad has two operations, pure and flatMap:

```scala
trait Monad[F[_]] extends Functor[F] {
  def flatMap[A, B](fa: F[A])(f: A => F[B]): F[B]
  def pure[A](x: A): F[A]
  def map[A, B](fa: F[A])(f: A => B): F[B] =
     flatMap(fa)(f andThen pure)
}
```

 Note that the category theory names for the `flatMap` operation is `bind`, and the name for `pure` is `unit`.

Recall from the previous section that you can think of Functors as a way to sequence operations on some type that preserves the structure of the type, as defined by the specificities of the type. Well, the same is true of a Monad, expect they're a bit more powerful. For Functors, the complications can only occur in the beginning of the sequence whereas with Monads, they can occur in any part of the sequence.

Let's look at an example:

```
Option(10).map(_ + 1).map(_ * 4)
res3: Option[Int] = Some(44)
```

What if one of the operations returned an Option?

```
def big(i: Int): Option[Int] =
  if (i > 5) Some(i)
  else None

big(10).map(_ - 5).map(big)
res3: Option[Option[Int]] = Some(None)
```

Now, we have a value of type `Option[Option[Int]]`, which isn't very convenient. This is where `Monad` comes in handy. If you have a sequence of operations where you want some specificities of some type to be preserved on every step, you'll want to use a `Monad`.

 As you can see from the preceding definition, a Monad is also a Functor, as map can be implemented in terms of `flatMap` and `pure`.

Here's how you can define a Monad for Option:

```
implicit val optionMonad = new Monad[Option] {
  def pure[A](x: A): Option[A] = Some(x)
  def flatMap[A, B](fa: Option[A])(f: A => Option[B]): Option[B] = fa
match {
    case Some(x) => f(x)
    case None => None
  }
}
```

`pure` is defined by simply wrapping the value in `Some`. `flatMap` is defined by pattern matching on the value and applying the function if it's `Some`, otherwise returning `None`.

We can avoid the previous inconvenient situation of having an `Option[Option[Int]]`:

```
flatMap(map(big(10))(_ - 5))(big)
```

We have seen the definition of the Monad and how it can be used to sequence operations in a specific context where each step in the sequence needs to preserve some specificities that depend on the instance of the Monad.

Popular Libraries

By this point, you should have a good understanding of the main concepts behind functional programming such as pure functions, immutability, and higher-order functions. In addition to that, you should be familiar with some of the most popular abstractions used when writing functional programs. With all of this knowledge, you are well equipped to start looking into some of the popular functional programming libraries in Scala.

In this section, we'll look at some of the popular functional programming libraries from the Scala ecosystem. After this section, you should be able to:

- Use the `Cats Validated` type class to validate your data
- Use `Doobie` to talk to databases

Validating Data Using Cats

In this section, we'll get a quick overview of the Cats library and look at one of the data types it provides to `Validate` data.

 For more information on Cats, refer to https://github.com/typelevel/cats.

By the end of this section, you should understand how `Cats` fits into the Scala ecosystem and know how to use it in your own projects, specifically to validate your data.

Prerequisites for Using Cats

1. You need to add `Cats` as a dependency to your Scala project. Create a new SBT project with the following `build.sbt` file:

```
name := "cats-example"

scalaVersion := "2.12.4"
libraryDependencies += "org.typelevel" %% "cats-core" % "1.0.0"

scalacOptions ++= Seq(
  "-Xfatal-warnings",
  "-Ypartial-unification"
)
```

2. As `Cats` relies heavily on implicits to provide type class instances and extension methods, you always need to have the following imports in your files when you're using `Cats`:

```
import cats._
import cats.implicits._
```

Introduction to Cats

Cats is a library which provides abstractions for functional programming in the Scala programming language. Specifically, it provides definitions for all of the patterns you saw in the previous section (Monoid, Monad, and so on) and many more. It also contains type class instances for all of the relevant classes from the Scala standard library.

The broader goal of Cats is to provide a foundation for an ecosystem of pure, typeful libraries to support functional programming in Scala applications.

Validating Data

There are two different ways to validate data using Cats. The first is `Either`, as you know it from the standard library, and the other is `Validated`. You should use `Either` if you want your validation to fail-fast and you should use `Validated` if you want to accumulate the errors. Which one you should use depends on your use case. As you might be familiar with `Either` from the standard library, we'll focus on `Validated` in this subsection.

First, let's have a look at a basic domain model and some constraints we have for the data. Let's assume you have a `User` that looks like the following:

```
final case class User(
  username: String,
  age: Int
)
```

Let's also assume that you have the following rules for this user:

- The username has to contain at least three characters.
- The username can only contain alphanumeric characters.
- The age has to be positive.

We can represent these three errors in Scala using a sealed trait with case objects like this:

```
sealed trait Error {
  def message: String
}

case object SpecialCharacters extends Error {
  val message: String = "Value can't contain special characters"
}

case object TooShort extends Error {
  val message: String = "Value is too short"
}

case object ValueTooLow extends Error {
  val message: String = "Value is too low"
}
```

Let's look at how we could write the preceding rules in Scala using `Validated`.

Validating Using Validated

The `Validated` data type is defined like this:

```
sealed abstract class Validated[+E, +A] extends Product with
Serializable
final case class Valid[+A](a: A) extends Validated[Nothing, A]
final case class Invalid[+E](e: E) extends Validated[E, Nothing]
```

Here, `Valid[A]` represents a value of type `A` that passed some kind of validation, and `Invalid[A]` represents that some validation failed, producing an error of type `E`. Let's try to implement the rules from the previous section:

```
def validateAge(age: Int): Validated[NonEmptyList[Error], Int] =
    if (age >= 1) age.validNel
    else ValueTooLow.invalidNel
```

Here, we define a method, `validateAge`, which takes an `Int` and returns `Validated[NonEmptyList[Error], Int]`, meaning that it will either return `Valid(age)` if it's valid or `Invalid(NonEmptyList(ValueTooLow))` if it's not. We use the extension methods `validNel` and `invalidNel` that `Cats` provides for your convenience.

Next up, let's define a validator for the username:

```
private def checkLength(str: String): Validated[NonEmptyList[Error],
String] =
  if (str.length > 3) str.validNel
  else TooShort.invalidNel

private def checkSpecialCharacters(str: String):
Validated[NonEmptyList[Error], String] =
  if (str.matches("^[a-zA-Z]+$")) str.validNel
  else SpecialCharacters.invalidNel

def validateUsername(username: String): Validated[NonEmptyList[Error],
String] =
  (checkLength(username), checkSpecialCharacters(username)).mapN {
    case (a, _) => a
  }
```

In this case, we're defining two helper functions, `checkLength` and
`checkSpecialCharacters`, which check that the string is longer than 3 characters
and doesn't contain any alphanumeric characters. We combine these two checks
using the `mapN` extension method that Cats provides on tuples. If both checks pass,
the `mapN` function will be invoked with a tuple containing both the valid values, but
we're only interested in the username once we simply return the first valid value.

Finally, let's write the method that validates both the username and the age and
returns a `User` if everything is valid:

```
def validate(username: String, age: Int) =
    (validateUsername(username), validateAge(age)).mapN { User.apply }
```

Again, we use the `mapN` method and pass in a function that should be invoked if
all checks pass. In this case, we use the `apply` method on `User` to create an instance
of `User`.

If you invoke this, you can see that it accumulates the errors if there are any;
otherwise, it returns a `User` that has been validated:

```
User.validate("!!", -1)
// Invalid(NonEmptyList(TooShort, SpecialCharacters, ValueTooLow))

User.validate("jack", 42)
// Valid(User(jack,42))
```

By now, you should know how to add Cats to your Scala projects and know how to use their `Validated` data type to write validation methods for your domain models in a nice, functional way. In the next section, we'll have a look at how to use the `Doobie` library to communicate with databases in a functional type-safe manner.

Communicating with Databases Using Doobie

In this subsection, we'll use the `Doobie` library to communicate with databases in a functional and type-safe manner. You will be introduced to the core concepts of `Doobie` and see how to use it to query, update, and delete rows in your database.

After this subsection, you should be able to use `Doobie` in your own Scala projects for simple queries and insertions, and know where to find documentation for more advanced use cases.

Prerequisites for Doobie

You need to add Doobie as a dependency to your Scala project. Create a new SBT project with the following `build.sbt` file:

```
scalaVersion := "2.12.4"

lazy val doobieVersion = "0.5.0-M13"

libraryDependencies ++= Seq(
  "org.tpolecat" %% "doobie-core"  % doobieVersion,
  "org.tpolecat" %% "doobie-h2"    % doobieVersion
)
```

Doobie can talk to many different databases, such as MySQL, Postgres, H2, and so on. In the following examples, we'll use the in-memory database H2 to simplify the setup. Have a look at the documentation to see how to use the other databases.

The database tables we'll use in these examples are quite simple. There are two tables, `user` and `todo`, which have the following SQL definitions:

```
CREATE TABLE user (
  userId INT AUTO_INCREMENT PRIMARY KEY,
  username VARCHAR(255) NOT NULL,
  age INT NOT NULL
);

CREATE TABLE todo (
  todoId INT AUTO_INCREMENT PRIMARY KEY,
  userId INT NOT NULL,
```

```
    title VARCHAR(255) NOT NULL,
    completed BOOL DEFAULT false,
    FOREIGN KEY (userId) references user(userId)
);
```

Doobie

In Doobie, to make large programs, you need to write small programs. After creating the program, you can directly drop it into your main function and use it as an effectful monad.

Doobie has a high-level and a low-level API. In this lecture, we'll focus exclusively on the high-level API. In the high-level API, there are only a handful of important classes. The two most important are ConnectionIO and Transactor.

ConnectionIO

The most common types you will deal with have the form ConnectionIO[A], specifying computations that take place in a context where a java.sql.Connection is available, ultimately producing a value of type A.

ConnectionIO[A] is the most common types you will come across, and it specifies the calculations that occur where java.sql.Connection is available, which generates a value of type A.

Transactor

A Transactor is a structure which is used for database connectivity, connection handouts, and cleanup; it can take a ConnectionIO[A] and produce an IO[A], which provides an executable code. It specifically provides you an IO that, when executed, will connect to the database and run the program in a single transaction.

Here's a full example that creates a Transactor that can connect to the H2 database. We then use that transactor to perform the simple query SELECT 42:

```
package com.example

import doobie._
import doobie.implicits._
import cats.effect.IO

object ExampleConnection extends App {

  val transactor =
    Transactor.fromDriverManager[IO](
```

```
        "org.h2.Driver", "jdbc:h2:mem:test", "", ""
    )
  val program: ConnectionIO[Int] =
      sql"select 42".query[Int].unique

  val task: IO[Int] =
    program.transact(transactor)

  val result: Int =
    task.unsafeRunSync

  println(s"Got result ${result}")

}
```

The preceding example creates a `Transactor` using `Transactor`. `fromDriverManager` and then creates a small program that, when provided with a `Connection`, will run `SELECT 42`. Finally, the program is turned into an `IO` monad using the transact method on `ConnectionIO`, and the `IO` monad is executed using `unsafeRunSync` to produce an `Int` that is the result of executing `SELECT 42`. It's important to understand that no side effects are occurring until the `IO` monad is executed using `unsfaceRunSync`.

Next up, let's have a look at how to write queries.

Selecting Rows

Now that we've seen how to use the `ConnectionIO` and `Transactor`, let's have a look at some more interesting queries to perform a very simply query.

Let's start by examining the following expression from the previous example:

```
val fragment: Fragment = sql"select 42"
val query: Query0[Int] = fragment.query[Int]
val program = query.unique
```

We use the Doobies string interpolation function `sql` to turn a normal `String` into a `Fragment`. A `Fragment` is simply Doobie's representation of parts of an SQL query, which may include interpolated values. `Fragments` can be composed by concatenation, which maintains the correct offset and mappings for interpolated values. In this lecture, we won't go into detail with what you can do with `Fragments`, but you can find more information in the documentation.

Once you have a `Fragment`, you can turn it into a `Query` using the `query[A]` method on `Fragment`. `Query[A, B]` is Doobie's representation for a complete SQL query that takes some input of type A and produces some output of type B. In this specific example, our query doesn't take any input, so the specific type `Query0` is returned, which represents a query that doesn't take any parameters.

Finally, a `ConnectionIO[Int]` is produced by using the `unique` method on `Query`. As stated previously, `ConnectionIO[A]` represents computations that take place in a context where a `java.sql.Connection` is available, ultimately producing a value of type A. In this case, we use `unique` as we're only expecting one row to be returned. Other interesting methods are `list` and `option`, which return `ConnectionIO[List[A]]` and `ConnectionIO[Option[A]]`, respectively.

Querying Using Parameters

In Doobie, you pass parameters to queries as you would with any string interpolator. The parameters are turned into ? expressions in prepared statements to avoid SQL injections. Let's have a look at how to query using parameters:

 You can find the following queries in `lesson-1/doobie-example/src/main/scala/com/example/User.scala`.

```scala
case class User(userId: Int, username: String, age: Int)

def allManual(limit: Int): ConnectionIO[List[User]] = sql"""
    SELECT userId, username, age
    FROM user
    LIMIT $limit
  """
    .query[(Int, String, Int)]
    .map { case (id, username, age) => User(id, username, age) }
    .list

def withUsername(username: String): ConnectionIO[User] = sql"""
    SELECT userId, username, age
    FROM user
    WHERE username = $username
  """.query[User].unique
```

The first query, `allManual`, takes an `Int` and uses it as a parameter to define the `LIMIT` of the SQL query. The second query takes a `String` and uses it in a `WHERE` clause to select users with that specific username. The `allManual` query selects a `Tuple` of (`Int`, `String`, `Int`) and maps over it to produce a `User`, whereas `withUsername` uses Doobie's ability to automatically use the `apply` method of a case class when querying for rows of that type.

Deleting, Inserting, and Updating Rows

Deleting, inserting, and updating works in a similar way. First, let's look at how to delete rows:

```
def delete(username: String): ConnectionIO[Int] = sql"""
   DELETE FROM user
   WHERE username = $username
 """.update.run
```

Again, we use the SQL string interpolator to define our query and simply refer to variables in scope to define parameters to the query. However, instead of using the `query[A]` method on `Fragment` to produce a `Query`, we use `update[A]` to produce an `Update[A]`. We then use the `run` method on `Update` to produce a `ConnectionIO[A]`:

```
def setAge(userId: Int, age: Int): ConnectionIO[Int] = sql"""
   UPDATE user
   SET age = $age
   WHERE userId = $userId
 """.update.run

def create(username: String, age: Int): ConnectionIO[Int] = sql"""
   INSERT INTO user (username, age)
   VALUES ($username, $age)
 """.update.withUniqueGeneratedKeys[Int]("userId")
```

Both `setAge` and `create` are similar, but `create` uses an interesting method on `Update` named `withUniqueGeneratedKeys`, which returns the `id` of the row that was inserted last.

A Complete Example

Let's have a look at a full example. You can find it in `lesson-1/doobie-example/` `src/main/scala/com/example/Main.scala`. We'll look at each section piece by piece:

```scala
val program = for {
    _    <- Tables.create
    userId <- User.create("Jack", 41)
    _ <- User.setAge(userId, 42)
    _ <- Todo.create(userId, "Buy Milk", false)
    _ <- Todo.create(userId, "Read the newspaper", false)
    _ <- Todo.create(userId, "Read the full documentation for Doobie",
false)
    uncompleted <- Todo.uncompleted(userId)
  } yield uncompleted
```

In this section, you can see how to chain `ConnectionIO` using `flatMap` through Scala `for-comprehensions`. This allows us to nicely construct `ConnectionIO` from the result of executing another `ConnectionIO`. In this case, we use it to first create a `User` and then use the `userId` in subsequent methods to set the user's age and construct three `Todo` methods for the user:

```scala
val all: IO[Unit] = for {
  todos <- program.transact(xa)
  users <- User.all(10).transact(xa)
} yield {
  todos.foreach(println)
  users.foreach(println)
}
```

In this section, we will produce `IO` from two `ConnectionIO` instances by using the `transact` method in a `for-comprehension`:

```scala
all.unsafeRunSync
```

Finally, the `IO` is executed to produce side effects.

Activity: Adding Priority to the Todo List

Imagine a scenario where a client has told you that he needs priority function added to his Todo lists. Design the priority for the application.

Extend the example program in `lesson-1/doobie-example` by adding a priority to each of the Todos and use the priority when querying for uncompleted todos so that the most important is returned first. You'll have to perform the following steps:

1. Extend the `Todo case class` with a `priority: Int` field.
2. Update the `Table` definition in `Todo.table`.
3. Update the `Todo.create` method to take an `Int` that represents the priority.
4. Update `Todo.uncompleted` so it orders the rows in descending order.

Summary

In this chapter, we covered the core concepts of functional programming like Pure functions, immutability, and higher-order functions. We introduced some of the design patterns that are prevalent in large functional programs. Finally, we covered two popular functional programming libraries called Cats and Doobie, and used them to write some interesting programs.

In the next chapter, we will cover how Scala makes it possible to write powerful Domain-Specific Languages (DSLs) by providing a few interesting language features. We'll have a brief look at what DSLs are in general terms. We'll also cover a DSL that you'll very likely be using if you're going to work with Scala professionally. Finally, you will implement your own DSL.

8

Domain Specific Languages

In the previous chapter, we covered the core concepts of functional programming such as pure functions, immutability, and higher-order functions. We introduced some of the design patterns that are prevalent in large functional programs. Finally, we covered two popular functional programming libraries called Cats and Doobie and used them to write some interesting programs.

In this chapter, we will cover how Scala makes it possible to write powerful DSLs by providing a few interesting language features. We'll have a brief look at what DSLs are in general terms. We'll also cover a DSL that you'll very likely be using if you're going to work with Scala professionally. Finally, you will implement your own DSL.

This chapter demonstrates how Scala makes it possible to write powerful Domain Specific Languages (DSLs) by providing a few interesting language features.

By the end of this chapter, you will be able to:

- Identify the use of Domain Specific Languages (DSLs)
- Use the DSL `ScalaTest`, a popular testing library for Scala
- Design your own DSLs in Scala
- Recognize the additional libraries and tools that will be useful beyond this book

DSLs and Types of DSLs

A domain specific language is, as the name suggests, a language that's specialized for a specific domain. Contrast that with a language like Scala, which is a general-purpose language in the sense that it's applicable across a broad range of domains.

By restricting the domain, you'd hope to make a language that's less comprehensive but better suited to solving a specific set of problems within a domain. A well-constructed DSL will make it easy to solve problems within a domain and make it hard for the user to make mistakes. DSLs come in many different shapes and sizes, but you can roughly separate them into two groups: external DSLs and internal DSLs.

External DSLs

External DSLs are written "outside" of the host language (the language that's used to implement the DSL is called the host language). That means you'll have to parse the text, evaluate it, and so on, just as if you were creating a general-purpose programming language. We won't be creating an external DSL, so we won't cover the topic much further.

One example of an external DSL is DOT, which is used to describe graphs. Here's an example of a simple DOT program, which produces the graph you see here:

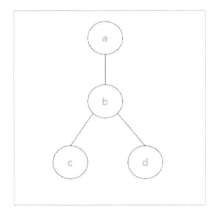

Here is the code that can be written to implement the graph above:

```
graph graphname {
    a -- b -- c;
    b -- d;
}
```

So, DOT is specialized for the domain of describing graphs.

For more information on DOT, please refer to https://
en.wikipedia.org/wiki/DOT_(graph_description_
language).

Internal DSLs

Internal DSLs are embedded in the host language and can be separated into two groups:

- **Shallow:** Operations directly use the host language's operations (for example, + uses Scala's +).
- **Deep:** You build up your abstract syntax tree (AST) and evaluate it just as you would with an external DSL.

We'll be writing an internal shallow DSL in this chapter, which is also, in my experience, the most common type of DSL you'll encounter when you're using various Scala libraries.

ScalaTest is a very popular testing library for Scala. It has a set of different DSLs for writing your test specifications. We'll look at ScalaTest in depth in the next section.

You now have a very basic understanding of what DSLs are and how they can be grouped into internal/external and shallow/deep. In the next section, we'll look at ScalaTest and how that library uses DSLs to make it easy to write test specifications.

ScalaTest – A Popular DSL

 ScalaTest was introduced in *Chapter 1, Setting up the Development Environment*, but as we'll use it extensively in this lecture, we'll do a little recap here and make sure that everyone has a working ScalaTest environment.

In this section, we'll have a look at a popular library for testing your Scala programs, ScalaTest, and see how the library uses DSLs to allow its users to write readable tests in various styles.

The purpose of looking at ScalaTest is twofold. First off, ScalaTest is a widely used testing library for Scala projects, so you're likely to end up using it when you're using Scala professionally. Secondly, it's a good example of how to use DSLs to make your code more readable.

By the end of this section, you should be able to:

- Identify how to use ScalaTest in your own projects
- Identify the various styles that ScalaTest offers and be able to pick the one that's relevant to your project
- Write ScalaTest tests using the FlatSpec style

Adding ScalaTest to Your Project

ScalaTest is a Scala library like any other, so you simply add it as a library dependency to your project. As we're using SBT in this book, we'll use that as an example here. Create a new SBT project with the following build.sbt file:

```
name := "Lession2-ScalaTest"
scalaVersion := "2.12.4"
libraryDependencies += "org.scalatest" %% "scalatest" % "3.0.4" %
"test"
```

 For more information, refer to the installation section (http://www.scalatest.org/install) from the documentation if you want to see how to use it outside of SBT.

Create a simple test and place it in your src/test/scala/com/example/ExampleSpec.scala project:

```
package com.example

import collection.mutable.Stack
import org.scalatest._

class ExampleSpec extends FlatSpec with Matchers {
  "A Stack" should "pop values in last-in-first-out order" in {
    val stack = new Stack[Int]
    stack.push(1)
    stack.push(2)
    stack.pop() should be (2)
    stack.pop() should be (1)
  }
}
```

To verify that your setup is correct, start an SBT session in the root of your project and run the following command:

```
test:compile                          # to compile your tests
test                                  # to run your test-suite
testOnly com.example.ExampleSpec # To run just that test
```

You should see output similar to the following:

```
testOnly com.example.ExampleSpec
[info] ExampleSpec:
[info] A Stack
[info] - should pop values in last-in-first-out order
[info] Run completed in 282 milliseconds.
[info] Total number of tests run: 1
[info] Suites: completed 1, aborted 0
[info] Tests: succeeded 1, failed 0, canceled 0, ignored 0, pending 0
[info] All tests passed.
[success] Total time: 6 s, completed Dec 4, 2017 9:50:04 PM
```

As we'll be writing a few tests using `ScalaTest` in the following section, it's important that you have a correctly configured SBT project that you can use for the exercises. Follow these steps:

1. Create a new SBT project using the previous `build.sbt` definition.
2. Create a new test file at `src/test/scala/com/example/ExampleSpec.scala` with the previous contents.
3. Run the tests using the `sbt test` command and make sure that it has detected the tests and that they pass.

You've seen how to add `ScalaTest` to your Scala project and how to run the tests using SBT. You should now have a correctly configured Scala project that you can use for the remainder of the exercises in this chapter. In the next section, we'll have a look at the various styles of tests you can write using `ScalaTest`.

Overview of ScalaTest Styles

ScalaTest offers a selection of different styles that you can use when you're writing your tests. What style to use depends on your team's experience and preference.

In this section, we'll have a look at some of the different styles so you can get a feeling for what style you prefer:

- **FunSuite** is a simple style that will be familiar to most people:

```
describe("A Set") {

  describe("(when empty)") {
    it("should have size 0") {

      assert(Set.empty.size == 0)

    }

  }

}
```

- **FlatSpec** is very similar to `FunSuite` but it focuses more on Behavior-Driven Design (BDD) by forcing you to name your tests in a manner that reads more like a specification:

```
"An empty Set" should "have size 0" in {

  assert(Set.empty.size == 0)

}
```

- **FunSpec** is a good general-purpose style for writing specification-style tests:

```
describe("A Set") {

  describe("(when empty)") {

    it("should have size 0") {

      assert(Set.empty.size == 0)

    }

  }

}
```

- **FreeSpec** focuses on specification-style testing but doesn't enforce any structure upon your tests:

```
"A Set" - {

  "(when empty)" - {

    "should have size 0" in {

      assert(Set.empty.size == 0)

    }

  }

}
```

- **PropSpec** is for if you want to write tests exclusively in terms of property checks:

```
property("An empty Set should have size 0") {

    assert(Set.empty.size == 0)

}
```

- **FeatureSpec** is primarily intended for acceptance testing:

```
class TVSetSpec extends FeatureSpec with GivenWhenThen {

  info("As a TV set owner")

  info("I want to be able to turn the TV on and off")



  feature("TV power button") {
    scenario("User presses power button when TV is off") {

      Given("a TV set that is switched off")

      val tv = new TVSet
```

```
      assert(!tv.isOn)

      When("the power button is pressed")

      tv.pressPowerButton()

      Then("the TV should switch on")

      assert(tv.isOn)

    }

  }

}
```

Example: `FunSuite`

Let's have a look at the test case we created in the previous section:

```
package com.example

import collection.mutable.Stack
import org.scalatest._

class ExampleSpec extends FlatSpec with Matchers {
  "A Stack" should "pop values in last-in-first-out order" in {
    val stack = new Stack[Int]
    stack.push(1)
    stack.push(2)
    stack.pop() should be (2)
    stack.pop() should be (1)
  }
}
```

There are two internal DSLs in action here. The first one is used to write your test specifications in the readable form of `"X" should "Y" in { <code> }`. This style is made available by extending `FlatSpec`. The other DSL is used to write your assertions in the form of `<expression> should be <expression>`, which is made available by extending `Matchers`.

The DSLs are implemented as a combination of classes and extension methods, but we'll look into that in greater detail when we implement our own little DSL in the next section.

Activity: Implementing ScalaTest Styles

The best way to get a feeling for the different styles is to use them. Select three of the styles from the previous list and convert the following test to those styles.

1. Continue using the Scala project you created in the previous activity.

2. Create a file for each style you've selected. If you picked `FunSpec`, then create a `FunSpecExample.scala` file.

3. For each style, convert the following test into a test that uses that style:

```scala
import collection.mutable.Stack
import org.scalatest._

class ExampleSpec extends FlatSpec with Matchers {
  "A Stack" should "pop values in last-in-first-out order" in {
    val stack = new Stack[Int]
    stack.push(1)
    stack.push(2)
    stack.pop() should be (2)
    stack.pop() should be (1)
  }
}
```

You've seen the different styles that `ScalaTest` offers and have a rough feeling for the difference between them.

`ScalaTest` is a testing library that uses DSLs to make it possible to write very readable tests. We have seen how you can add it to your own Scala projects, we got an overview of the different styles that it supports, and we have written a few tests using different styles. In the next section, we'll look at the Scala features that Scala provides which make it possible to write DSLs in Scala.

Language Features for Writing DSLs

In this section, we'll look at the Scala features that make it easy to write small DSLs:

- Flexible syntax for method invocation
- By-name parameters
- Extension methods and `Value` classes

We'll use all of these features in the next section when we create our own DSL in Scala.

Flexible Syntax for Method Invocation

Scala has a flexible syntax for method invocations that makes it possible to, in some cases, omit the dot (`.`) and parentheses (`()`) when invoking methods.

The rules are as follows:

- For methods that are of arity-`0`, meaning they don't take any parameters, the parentheses can be omitted and you can use the postfix notation.
- For methods with an arity of `1` or more, meaning they take one or more parameters, it's possible to write the method using infix notation.

Here's an example of using infix notation when invoking `filter`:

```
List.range(0, 10).filter(_ > 5)
List.range(0, 10) filter (_ > 5)
```

And here's an example of omitting the parentheses when invoking `toUpperCase`:

```
"Professional Scala".toUpperCase()
"Professional Scala".toUpperCase
```

This allows you to write code that reads more like prose, which is a nice option to have when you're creating your DSL.

By-Name Parameters

By-name parameters make it possible to specify that a parameter that's passed to a function shouldn't be evaluated until it's actually used:

```
def whileLoop(condition: => Boolean)(body: => Unit): Unit =
  if (condition) {
    body
    whileLoop(condition)(body)
  }

var i = 2

whileLoop (i > 0) {
 println(i)
 i -= 1
}  // prints 2 1
```

Note that both the `condition` and `body` parameter types have a `=>` prepended. That's how you specify that a parameter is a by-name parameter.

We'll use by-name parameters to enable the user to write the ... in { ... code ... } blocks for the tests cases when we're writing our own DSL later in this chapter.

 It's important to note that by-name parameters are evaluated every time they're referenced.

Extension Methods and Value Classes

Extension methods are a technique for adding new methods to already existing Scala classes. Value Classes is a Scala feature that, among other things, makes it possible to create extension methods without incurring any allocation overhead.

Here's an example of a Value class that adds an extension method to String:

```
implicit class StringExtensions(val self: String) extends AnyVal {
  def repeat(count: Int): String =
    List.range(0, count).map(_ => self).fold("")(_ + _)
}
```

With this definition, there will be an implicit conversion from String to StringExtension, which allows you to invoke repeat on a string as if it had always been there (note the use of the postfix notation):

```
"Professional Scala" repeat 5
```

We'll use extension methods and Value classes to add the should method to String when we're writing our own DSL later in this chapter.

We've seen how Scala's features make it possible to write nice internal DSLs in Scala. We'll now see how to write a custom DSL.

Writing a Small DSL

In this section, we'll reimplement some FlatSpec ScalaTest DSLs in order to see how to implement DSLs in Scala.

First, we'll have a look at a simple way to model test cases in Scala using case classes. Then, we'll have a look at how to create a little DSL for creating those test cases.

Modeling Test Cases

Before we can create a DSL, we need to have something to create a DSL for. In our case, we want to create a DSL for specifying tests, so let's have a look at how we could model tests using case classes in Scala:

```
sealed trait TestResult
case class TestFailure(message: String) extends TestResult
case object TestSuccess extends TestResult
```

We'll create an algebraic data type that represents the result of running a test case. The result can either be a failure that contains a message regarding the failure, or a TestSuccess that simply indicates that the test passed:

```
case class TestCase(description: TestDescription, run: () =>
TestResult)
case class TestDescription(name: String, specification: String)
```

Then, we define two simple case classes. TestDescription contains the description of a test case, whereas TestCase has such a description and a run function that can be used to invoke the test case.

With this simple model, we can describe a test case like the following:

```
TestCase(
    TestDescription("A stack", "pop values in last-in-first-out
order"),
    TestResult.wrap({
        val stack = new Stack[Int]
        stack.push(1)
        stack.push(2)
        assert(stack.pop() == 2, "should be (2)")
        assert(stack.pop() == 1, "should be (1)")
    })
)
```

Here, TestResult.wrap is a method with the signature def wrap(body: =>
Unit): () => TestResult.

Now, this looks nothing like the nice test cases we wrote in the previous section using the FlatSpec DSL, so let's have a look at how we can create a DSL that creates a TestCase like the previous one.

DSL for TestCase

We'll start by looking at the part of the DSL that makes it possible to write the test specification, that is, the part of the DSL shown here:

```
"A Stack (with one item)" should "be non-empty" in { … code … }
```

From the last section, it should be clear that this is using an extension method `should` on `String` that's invoked using infix notation. So, we'll add an extension method to `String` to create `TestDescription` using the little DSL from before:

```
implicit class StringExtension(val name: String) extends AnyVal {
  def should(specification: String): TestDescription =
    TestDescription(name, specification)
}
```

With this implicit value class in scope, we can create a `TestDescription` using the following syntax:

```
"A Stack (with one item)" should "be non-empty"
// Returns TestDescription("A Stack (with one item)","be non-empty")
```

This reduces our `TestCase` creation to the following.

```
TestCase(
    "A Stack (with one item)" should "be non-empty"
    TestResult.wrap({
        val stack = new Stack[Int]
        stack.push(1)
        stack.push(2)
        assert(stack.pop() == 2, "should be (2)")
        assert(stack.pop() == 1, "should be (1)")
    })
)
```

This is slightly better, but far from ideal. Let's continue. Now, let's focus on the remaining part of the DSL, the part that makes it possible to write the actual test case. It's the part of the DSL shown here:

```
"A Stack (with one item)" should "be non-empty" in { … code … }
```

Again, in the previous section, we saw that we could write such expressions in Scala using infix notation and by-name parameters. Now, to allow the creation of `TestCase` instances using the DSL, we'll have to add a method to `TestDescription` as follows:

```
def in(body: => Unit): TestCase = TestCase(this, TestResult.
wrap(body))
```

With this method, we can now write our test case using the following syntax:

```
"A Stack (with one item)" should "be non-empty" in {
    val stack = new Stack[Int]
    stack.push(1)
    stack.push(2)
    assert(stack.pop() == 2, "should be (2)")
    assert(stack.pop() == 1, "should be (1)")
}
```

And, with that, we're done with creating our little DSL for writing test case specifications.

We're not trying to create a full-featured testing library here, but it would be fun to be able to run the tests, so let's have a look at how to implement a test runner.

As we've modeled our test cases using Scala classes, it's quite simple to create a test runner that runs the tests and prints a nice little report.

You've seen how to use some of Scala's features to very easily write a DSL to create test cases. By using the flexible syntax for method invocation, by-name parameters, and extension methods (through Value classes), you've managed to create an internal DSL that makes it possible to convert this expression:

```
TestCase(
    TestDescription("A stack", "pop values in last-in-first-out
order"),
    TestResult.wrap({
        val stack = new Stack[Int]
        stack.push(1)
        stack.push(2)
        assert(stack.pop() == 2, "should be (2)")
        assert(stack.pop() == 1, "should be (1)")
    })
)
```

Into the following:

```
"A Stack" should "pop values in last-in-first-out order" in {
    val stack = new Stack[Int]
  stack.push(1)
  stack.push(2)
  assert(stack.pop() == 2, "should be (2)")
  assert(stack.pop() == 1, "should be (1)")
}
```

Activity: Creating a DSL to Specify Assertions

Our DSL makes it possible to write TestCase instances easily. However, the assertions in our test cases don't look very nice. Create a DSL to specify assertions. It should support the following syntax:

```
expected(2) from stack.pop()
```

Hint:

Start by modeling assertions using case classes:

```
case class Assertion[A](expected: Expected[A], value: () => A)
case class Expected[A](expected: A)
```

 You can see the final result in the code for this chapter in dsl/src/main/scala/com/example/Assertion. scala and the usage in dsl/src/main/scala/com/example/Assertion.scala/Main.scala.

The full code should look like this:

```
package com.example

case class Assertion[A](expected: Expected[A], value: () => A) {
  def run(): Unit = {
    val result = value()
    assert(expected.expected == result, s"Failed asserting that ${expected.expected} == $result")
  }
}
case class Expected[A](expected: A) {
  def from(expression: => A): Assertion[A] = Assertion(
    this,
```

```
      () => expression
  )
}

object Assertion {

  def expected[A](x: A): Expected[A] = Expected(x)

}
```

Beyond This Book

This section will help you get a better overview of the Scala ecosystem and help guide your self-study after the book has ended, so you can continue to improve your Scala skills.

Various Scala Libraries

The purpose of this topic is to briefly introduce a couple of different Scala libraries for solving problems in different domains so that you can study the ones that are interesting to you after the book.

Akka

The first library we'll look at is one of the most popular libraries in the Scala ecosystem. It has been around for a long time — the first public release of the library was in 2010 — and it's used in production by a large number of big organizations.

Its main abstractions are Actor and Streams:

- Actors are a way to model concurrency without resorting to locks. You might have heard about them before if you've read about the programming language Erlang. An Actor is an entity that can receive and react to messages, spawn new actors, and send messages to other actors. Thus, you model your programs as a set of actors that communicate to each other by sending messages.

 You can find more information about Actors here: https://doc.akka.io/docs/akka/current/guide/actors-intro.html?language=scala

- If you have to deal with streaming data, you can use Akka `Streams` to model your programs as transformations over data flowing from sources into sinks.

 You can read more about `Streams` here: `https://doc.akka.io/docs/akka/current/stream/stream-introduction.html?language=scala`.

- If you want to build a distributed system in Scala, it is highly recommended to use Akka.

 You can read more about Akka on its website: `https://akka.io/`.

Apache Spark

Apache Spark is a library for processing large Scala datasets. Apache Spark was initially developed at UC Berkeley in 2009, and in 2013 it was donated to the Apache Software Foundation and is now a Top-Level Apache Project with more than 1,000 contributors.

You can write Spark programs in Java, Scala, Python, and R. You can write your own custom data analytics programs using the Spark API, or you can use one of the high-level APIs: Spark SQL for SQL and structured data processing, MLlib for machine learning, GraphX for graph processing, and Spark Streaming.

If you're interested in big data processing, take a look at Spark.

 You can read more about Spark on its website: `https://spark.apache.org/`.

Shapeless

Shapeless is a type class and dependent type-based generic programming library for Scala. It was initially written in 2011 by Miles Sabin and is now used by many companies to write type-safe code. It is also used internally by many libraries.

One of the major features of Shapeless is that it enables automatic derivation of type classes.

Using Shapeless, you can get the compiler to type-check things that you might not have thought possible. Some examples are:

- Heterogeneous lists, that is, lists where each element can be of different types and where the Scala compiler keeps track of the types
- Have the compiler check that collections are of a given length

In this section, we've seen three different Scala libraries that can be used to solve problems in the following domains:

- Distributed programming
- Big data processing
- Generic programming

Uncovered Language Features

The purpose of this topic is to briefly introduce you to some of the language features that we haven't covered, and show you where to go if you want to learn more about these topics. These features are:

- Macros
- Reflection

Macros

Macros are a programming language feature that makes it possible to write functions that take the AST of their arguments as input and produce a new AST, effectively allowing you to write programs that generate other programs.

Macros come in many shapes and sizes. In this section, we'll have a look at how to use macros in Scala. Experimental support for Scala macros was shipped with Scala 2.10, and, since then, they have been improved with every release.

 You can find the official documentation for macros on the Scala documentation website here: https://docs.scala-lang.org/ overviews/macros/overview.html.

Def Macros

Def macros are macros that are defined as Scala functions which reference a macro implementation. Let's have a look at a very simple macro that takes a `String` and returns an uppercase version of that string:

```
object Macros {

  def uppercaseImpl(c: Context)(strExpr: c.Expr[String]):
c.Expr[String] = {
    import c.universe._
    val Literal(Constant(str: String)) = strExpr.tree
    c.Expr[String](q"${str.toUpperCase}")
  }

  def uppercase(strExpr: String): String = macro uppercaseImpl
}
```

The `uppercase` method is how the macro is exposed to the users of the macro. The actual macro implementation is `uppercaseImpl`, which has two parameter lists. The first parameter contains a single argument, the `Context`, which contains information collected by the compiler at the call site of the macro. The second parameter contains the Scala abstract syntax trees of the expression of type `String` that the macro was invoked with. Let's see how to invoke this macro:

```
val x = Macros.uppercase("testing")
println(x)
```

This looks very much like a normal Scala method invocation; however, the uppercasing of the argument happens at compile time.

Note that the macro as implemented here only works with `String` literals; if you invoke it with anything else, you'll crash the compiler.

Implicit Macros

Implicit macros make it possible to reference a macro in the implementation of an implicit method. One use case of this is to write macros that can generate an instance of a given type class, given any type `T`:

```
trait Showable[T] { def show(x: T): String }
```

Then, instead of writing individual type class instances for all of your types, like the following:

```
final case class Person(name: String)

object Person {
 implicit val showable: Showable[Person] = new Showable[Person]{
   def show(x: Person) = s"Person(name=${x.name})"
 }
}
```

You could instead define an implicit macro that can generate an instance of the type class for any given type T, as follows:

```
object Showable {
 implicit def materializeShowable[T]: Showable[T] = macro ...
}
```

Quasiquotes

It is possible for you to use Scala's powerful String Interpolation feature to make it to write ASTs inside of Strings, so you don't have to construct the ASTs by hand. That is, you can write the following:

```
q"List(10)"
```

Instead of writing the following:

```
List(Literal(Constant(10)))))
```

Reflection

You have very likely used reflection in other programming languages, such as Java or Python. Reflection makes it possible for a program to inspect and sometimes modify itself. You can think of macros as compile-time reflection and of the reflections we'll look at now as runtime reflection.

With runtime reflection, you can:

- Inspect the types of objects
- Instantiate new objects
- Access or invoke members of an object

Let's have a look at an example of how to inspect types at runtime:

```scala
import scala.reflect.runtime.{universe => ru}

def getTypeTag[T: ru.TypeTag](obj: T) = ru.typeTag[T]

getTypeTag(List(1,2,3)).tpe.decls
  .filter(_.name.toString.length < 5)
  .foreach(d => println(s"${d.name} : ${d.typeSignature}"))
```

This example uses `scala.reflect.runtime.universe` to implement a method that, for a given object of type `T`, will get the `TypeTag` for that type. Given the `TypeTag`, we can access `Type` through `tpe` and then get the list of the members of the type through `decls`. The example then filters out any member whose name is shorter than five characters and prints their `name` and `type`.

 Reflection can in some cases incur a non-negligible runtime overhead. If you're using it in performance-sensitive places, make sure to benchmark the results.

In this subsection, we've briefly covered two interesting Scala language features and provided multiple links for further study of these features so that you can improve your Scala skills after this book.

Resources to Keep You Updated

In this subsection, we'll have a look at how you can keep up to date with the development of the Scala programming language, as well as its ecosystem.

Scala Improvement Process

The Scala Improvement Process (SIP) and Scala Platform Process (SPP) are how changes are made to the Scala Programming Language and The Scala Standard Library, respectively. If you want to make a change to either, you can make a proposal for the change, which will then be reviewed and potentially accepted.

 You can find a list of all the current SIPs here: https://docs.scala-lang.org/sips/all.html.

Scala Times

The Scala Times is a weekly newsletter that features interesting blog posts about Scala and gives a short recap of the various Scala libraries that have been released in the previous week.

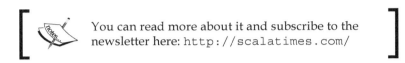 You can read more about it and subscribe to the newsletter here: http://scalatimes.com/

Summary

In this chapter, we covered how Scala makes it possible to write powerful Domain Specific Languages (DSLs) by providing a few interesting language features. We had a brief look at what DSLs are in general terms. We have also covered a DSL that you'll very likely be using if you're going to work with Scala professionally. Finally, we have implemented our own DSL.

We now come to the end of this book. In this book, we covered all the professional concepts of the Scala language, from setting up the development environment to writing your own custom DSLs. We covered the object-oriented and functional programming aspects of the Scala language. We also covered some useful libraries that are used in Scala, such as Cats and Doobie. Finally, we covered the additional resources and tools that will help you to stay up to date in the industry.

Index

A

abstract type members 97

Actors
URL 152

advanced types
about 97
abstract type members 97
structural types 98

Akka
about 152
URL 153

AnyRef 88

Any type
about 88
AnyRef 88
AnyVal 88

AnyVal 88

Apache Spark
about 153
URL 153

B

base syntax, Scala
about 12
for definitions 13
for expressions 14, 15

basic sbt commands
sbt compile 8
sbt run 8

binary search tree
implementation, generalizing 92

binary search tree implementation
generalizing 93

bottom type 88

bounds 90

by name parameter passing mode 48

by-name parameters 146

by need parameter passing mode 49

by value parameter passing mode 48

C

category theory 120

Cats library
about 126, 127
data validation, with Validated data
type 128, 129
prerequisites 126
reference link 126
used, for data validation 126-128

chatbot
ConsoleOutput, implementing 40
DefaultTimeProvider, implementing 40
environment and logic, decoupling 38, 39
OO, implementing in 38
simple TODO-list, adding 70

ChatbotMode
representing, as partial function 64

www.ingramcontent.com/pod-product-compliance
Lightning Source LLC
Chambersburg PA
CBHW080529060326
40690CB00022B/5077